# Families of Two

# Families of Two

### Interviews With
### Happily Married Couples
### Without Children by Choice

❀

## Laura Carroll

### Photographs by Krista Bartz

Library of Congress Number:     00-191087
ISBN #:          Hardcover      0-7388-2261-2
                 Softcover      0-7388-2262-0

This book was printed in the United States of America.

To order additional copies of this book, contact:
Xlibris Corporation
1-888-7-XLIBRIS
www.Xlibris.com
Orders@Xlibris.com

# Contents

*For*
*Michael*

# ACKNOWLEDGEMENTS

*M*any wonderful people made this book possible. I would like to thank all of the people who responded to my advertisements and letters in my search for couples to participate in this project. Many thanks to the couples who agreed to be interviewed. I appreciate and respect their willingness to share their thoughts and feelings.

I interviewed more than thirty interesting couples leading fulfilling lives, and it was difficult to choose the interviews to include in this book. My deepest thanks goes to the couples who agreed to have their interview excerpts and photographs be part of this book. They took the time to be interviewed and photographed, and to review excerpts I selected. I am honored to be the mid-wife of their words.

This book has also given me the opportunity to work with Krista Bartz. In the early phases of this project, I saw her photography in the literary magazine, *The Sun.* I was so impressed that I wasted no time in finding her and pitching her on this project. I admire her creativity and diligence.

Loving thanks to my dear friends who encourage me in my endeavors. I want to extend special thanks to the group of women friends without children who sat in my living room one night before I decided to pursue this project. I invited them over to talk about marriage without children. Through them, I began to learn how much there is to say on this topic, and I became even more inspired to find couples to learn more from.

I also want to thank editor Katherine Hyatt of oureditor.com for her editorial savvy and enthusiasm for this book.

My deepest gratitude goes to my husband, Michael, my lifelong love.

$\backsim 9 \backsim$

# INTRODUCTION

*O*n our eleventh wedding anniversary, my husband and I found ourselves looking to the future. We loved each other, and were enjoying the life we had created together, but we asked ourselves: Will this be enough glue for a lifelong marriage?

We saw how parenthood became serious glue for couples we knew and how it deepened the purpose of their marriage, but unlike just about every couple we knew, we had decided not to have children. We knew very few couples like us, and didn't know any who had been married a long time and chosen not to parent. We wondered where we could find them to learn about road maps for lifelong marriage without children.

I looked for books on married couples who did not have children by choice. While I found many books on how to have a successful marriage, few if any, addressed the topic of marriage without parenthood. I found a number of books that focused on "childlessness" and being "childfree," but most of them focused only on women's experiences. A number of books dealt with couples who ended up without children because they could not have them and chose not to adopt. A few books dealt with marriage without children, but they either were out of print, or published some time ago. I did not find any books that looked into the lives of happily married couples without children by choice.

I dug deeper, went to the research literature, and found many studies on voluntary or intentional childlessness. I learned more about what research tells us about the characteristics of those who choose not to parent, and common reasons for making this decision. While interesting, I still wanted to know: Where are real examples of long-time, happily married couples who chose not to parent? What are their lives like? How do they "do" their marriage? What would they say has made their marriage last?

My quest for these answers inspired me to create a book, profiling "happily ever after" couples without children by choice. I began to explore the idea by inviting a group of married women who did not have children into my home to talk about marriage without children. From the moment I turned on the tape recorder, the conversation flowed. We covered a range of topics, from how we made our choice, and how others see us, to the chapters of our marriages. As I listened to these women, I got excited. How much they had to say—how much I could learn!

Inspired, I set out to find couples to interview. I wanted to talk with happily married couples who had been married at least ten years, had no children from their current or previous relationships, and had chosen not to have children. First, I sent a letter that explained my project to family and friends, and asked them if they could help me find couples who fit the profile.

Even before I met with one couple, my learning began. My mother told me she was not going to ask her friends if they knew couples who fit the target profile. In fact, she wasn't going to tell them about the idea at all. She felt that her friends already thought it was strange that she was not a grandmother; now they would judge her further because her daughter wanted to do a book on couples that did not want children!

I had no idea my mother would react this way. However, what started as an uncomfortable conversation between us made us closer. Before then, we had not talked about why I did not want to have children. She told me that she sometimes wondered if it had something to do with what she did, or did not do, as a mother—that if she had mothered "better," I would have wanted children. I told her that she is a

*Laura Carroll*

great mom, and that I feel fortunate and thankful that I was raised to be independent, and to believe I could live my life in my own way.

I learned a lot about my mother's feelings about herself as a mother, and about her experience with her friends when it came to grandchildren. We talked about how she often feels left out when she gets together with her friends who are grandmothers, and how the conversation focuses almost exclusively on the grandchildren. I knew how she felt. Sharing our feelings helped us understand each other better, and deepened our bond.

Meanwhile, other family and friends gave me a few leads on couples to contact. Next, I put a display ad in my local newspaper. I received at least 100 calls from the ad and met with as many couples as I could that fit the profile.

Most often, I met with couples at their homes, and interviewed them for about two hours. With their permission, I taped their interviews for later transcription. Although I asked most of the same questions in each interview, all of the couples had their own stories to tell. One woman summed up the feelings of many of the couples: "Finally, someone wants to hear from us!"

After I had met with a number of couples in my local area, I advertised in different cities. I traveled to California, New York, and Connecticut, where respondents clustered the most. As the number of couples I interviewed grew, I began to focus on finding more couples from different ethnic backgrounds. I advertised in newspapers with different ethnic readerships in the San Francisco Bay Area. I had lived there for fifteen years, so I knew the area. I ran most of the display ads three times and received very little response.

Frustrated, I went to Census data and found that the percentages of African-American and Hispanic women without children are quite low. Both percentages are lower than that for Caucasian women. It was hard to find out just how low the percentages are for each group because the data do not differentiate between women who had chosen not to have children and those who did not have them for other reasons, e.g., fertility issues. In any case, I wondered if I was having a hard time finding couples of different ethnicities who fit the profile because there aren't many of them, or because I had just advertised in the wrong places.

Despite these questions, by that time I had interviewed over thirty couples from a wide range of backgrounds and decided to select fifteen that best represent what I had learned from all of those with whom I talked. I wanted to present "real talk from real couples," and for them to be heard as they wished to be heard, without bias on my part. I excerpted portions of the interviews and then asked each couple to review and agree to the content for publication.

Couples also agreed to have their photographs taken. Photographer Krista Bartz and I wanted to stray from portrait shots, and we attempted to capture couples "in" their lives, doing things they enjoy. Interviews and photos combined, the result is a look into their lives and their thoughts on marriage without children.

As you will see, some themes emerged with the couples I interviewed. As Joan Offerman-Zuckerberg describes those who are voluntarily childless in *Gender in Transition,* they are a "diversified, individualistic group, not a homogeneous one." At the same time, I saw certain similarities between them that dispelled many of the myths commonly associated with people who choose not to have children.

Contrary to the notion that couples without children lack maturity, or are unwilling to take on the responsibilities of adulthood, the couples I interviewed take their decisions and responsibilities seriously. Like all big decisions they make or responsibilities they choose to take on, they very carefully considered their decision about parenthood. They realistically looked at how having children would affect their lives and what it would truly mean to them individually and as a couple. All of them are leading adult lives and handling the responsibilities that often come with it, e.g., working at jobs, running businesses, paying mortgages, etc.

The couples arrived at their decision in a variety of ways. Contrary to what society tends to espouse, they did not make their decision

*Laura Carroll*

because they do not like children. Most of those with whom I talked would not say they dislike children. A few said that they feel uncomfortable around infants and that they feel more comfortable with children as the children get older. Virtually all of them feel they have a role to play in molding the next generation of children. A number of them work in professions that contribute to children, from teaching to matching nannies to the right families. Some are very involved with the children in their extended families, and others have relationships with children in their neighborhoods or churches. They tend to feel that it is very important for them to lead by example, and that they can fulfill their urge to nurture in many ways other than through biological offspring. They tend to like or even love children—they just don't want them as the main theme of their lives.

Also contrary to what people commonly believe, the female spouse did not solely drive the decision; many of the male spouses definitely had their minds set on not having children. In some cases, spouses came to their own individual realization before they were married; for others, the decision came gradually after they were married. Most often, at least initially, one spouse felt stronger than the other about not having children. Sometimes, the wife felt stronger about it and sometimes the husband.

Many of the couples did not get clear on the issue of children before they married. Some went into the marriage unsure about it and were willing to let the decision evolve over time. Only with a few couples I interviewed did one spouse want children when they married, and subsequently changed his or her mind along the way.

Overall, the couples deeply value their freedom and independence, and feel the responsibility of raising children would greatly limit these aspects of their lives. Like all of us, they have a desire to live the kind of life that suits them best. For this group, parenthood does not fit into the type of life they want. Many of them, especially the men with whom I met, don't care much about what others think of them or their lifestyles. Others may care more what people think, but it does not outweigh their desire to live their lives in their own way.

These people tend not to let others' or society's expectations stop them from doing what they want to do.

Many of the couples spoke of their concern about how having children would affect their relationship with each other. In fact, some said that having children would change the relationship forever, that they did not want this, and/or that they did not trust that having children would change the marriage in a positive direction. When making their decision on children, many of them decided that having a family was not worth the risk of potentially jeopardizing a very satisfying marital relationship.

Some couples expressed doubts about their abilities to parent because of their family histories or own childhood experiences, but their pasts could have easily been the pasts of parents. I interviewed people who come from happy families and others who come from less happy families. Just like many parents in today's society, some come from divorced families, and some had one or more alcoholic parent(s), but similar personal histories can influence very different futures.

Some people with less-than-perfect family histories can become motivated to "be the parents they never had," and, despite the parental modeling they received, believe they will be good parents. For others, their histories can play a big part in what motivates them *not* to want to become parents.

The couples with whom I talked also shattered the myth that people without children by choice are selfish, self-absorbed people. Most of them feel that, at one point or another, others, especially parents, have probably seen them as selfish for not having children, but they have varying views on what being selfish means, and why they consider themselves selfish or not. In getting to know them, I saw these couples as anything but selfish. Most of them impressed me as seeing far beyond themselves, and as being very aware of how their actions affect others, their communities, and our world. Many couples spoke of population, environmental, and social concerns, and are out there making a difference, from living an environmentally con-

*Laura Carroll*

scious life, to volunteering their time and skills to children, the eld-
erly, their community, and people in other countries. They value and
find it rewarding to give back in these ways.

Like all of us, these couples want and seek fulfilling lives. It's just
that they don't believe they need to raise children to find fulfillment.
This belief goes against the strongly held notion that "you are not
complete unless you have a child." However, for these couples, there
are many ways to feel "complete." For them, children are not essential
to their happiness or sense of self-worth. Many of those with whom I
talked are very committed to self-awareness, personal growth, and
living a meaningful life. They may see parenting as a valuable growth
opportunity—just not one for them. Many of them feel that not having children permits greater opportunities for them to pursue their
individual and shared life goals, and some of them tend to see parenthood as a distraction from this quest. A few couples spoke of times
when they felt unsure about the direction of their lives and contem-
plated having children because it could have been an easy way to take
the spotlight off more existential questions they had about meaning
and purpose in their lives.

I also talked with the couples about the notion that people who
choose not to have children are different from everyone else. Most of
them do think they are different in some ways. Many of them tend to
see themselves as less religious and more independent, and to value
their freedom more than most people do. Some of them also tend to
believe they are less social than the average person. Others tend to
feel they are less materialistic and less concerned with going after the
"trappings" commonly associated with success. They see themselves
as not living their lives "by checklist," e.g., go to college, get the job,
get married, and buy the car, the house, the white picket fence, etc.

I observed some characteristics about the couples that could differentiate them from others, and, while informative, they can't be
taken as conclusive. Some, but not all, of the women had atypical,
untraditional mother role models. A number of the women had an
influential woman in their lives who either did not have children, or

had they lived in a different time, they would not have had them. Some of the men had lacking father role models, due either to physical or emotional absence. A good share of the men and women characterize themselves as the "responsible" or "rebellious" child in the family growing up. More of them are the oldest child, the youngest child, or the only child in their families. A small number of them had a wide gap between them and their next oldest sibling, such that they felt they grew up as an only child.

Unlike another common belief about people without children, the couples with whom I met come from varied socioeconomic backgrounds. The common picture of couples without children tends to show upper-middle-class people, and women who choose their career over motherhood. I interviewed mostly middle-class couples, and while some of the women are dedicated to their careers, other women would not say it is the reason they decided not to have children.

The way they set up their day-to-day lives looks untraditional in some ways. For example, some couples do not adhere to typical gender roles in their relationship. Most of the couples share the domestics. In many cases, men do their share of things, like the cleaning and laundry. A number of the women play typical "male" roles, from being the main breadwinner, to taking the lead on house repair projects or yard work.

Like most households, most of the couples have animal companions. By far, cats are the most popular with this group, and many of the couples have at least two of them. Some people see their animals as their "children," in some ways, and others definitely do not.

The couples have a variety of friends, some of which are parents, and some are not. They have had varied experiences with friends who have children. Some couples have found it difficult to maintain the friendships with couples who become parents, because they do not have children in common. Still others feel they have had a more difficult time finding friends because they do not have children.

Their marriages, as the central priority in their lives, drive their

*Laura Carroll*

lifestyles in many ways. It is very important to them to do things together, to share hobbies and interests. Many of them talked about how essential it is to have time to nurture the relationship and how they value the time they have to do this. However, time together did not come easy for all of them. A few couples talked about how their job demands and other responsibilities challenge them to spend as much time as they would like together.

I also asked couples about their views on the institution of marriage today. Some talked about the strong social expectation to have children and how they see it changing. Many tend to see marriage as more about partnership than procreation. As one woman put it, it is more about "connection, and one's commitment to that connection," than it is about having a family in the traditional sense. Although not always recognized as such, the couples see the two of them as a family unit. A number of couples would like society to recognize and accept different forms of family, such as the two of them, a connected group of friends, or same-sex relationships.

Yet, like definitions of family, not having children by choice often still puts people in what one woman called the "tributaries" of mainstream society. As Leslie Lafayette says in *Why Don't You Have Kids,* we "may be living in the most pronatalistic period of our society." Society puts great pressure on us to reproduce these days. Biological mothering and fathering is far more recognized and prided than all the other forms non-biological nurturing can take. In our society, parenthood is one of the most celebrated parts of life.

I hope the voices in this book will help people recognize, understand, and celebrate a life that looks different from what is most common today. I also hope it will help couples feel freer to make the decision not to have children, if this is what they truly want. I want the book to help people better understand those who choose not to have children, and that a lack of desire does not stem from something they lack. It is just about differences in desires and choices.

∗∗∗

I began working on this book knowing I did not want children, and ended the project even clearer about my decision. As far back as I can remember, I never felt a strong desire to be a mother. As a girl, I don't remember liking to play with baby dolls. Instead I played "family" with Barbie dolls, I believe, as a way to act out my emotions, confusions, and issues related to my own family experience. As a teenager, I baby-sat and did not like it. In high school, when I thought about my future, motherhood never occurred to me. I knew I wanted to go to college, and spent my late teens and early twenties completing undergraduate and graduate degrees in psychology.

As I reached my mid-twenties, I began to ask myself why I seemed to feel different than most of my friends about eventually wanting to become a parent. I pondered the societal notion that maybe I was the one with the problem. I certainly had other problems during this time. I felt confused about my career and got depressed. I started seeing a therapist and began digging into my past. Some things I learned about myself seemed to relate to my lack of desire to have children.

As a child, I saw my father as the one who had the power in my parents' relationship and in our family. Somehow, I got the message that if I were going to get anywhere in life, I needed to be more like my father. I headed in that direction, and by the time I was twenty-five, I was unhappy but did not know why. Over time, I began to understand. Big parts of myself were locked away somewhere inside. I needed to unravel my over-masculinized persona, and unlock and embrace the feminine side in me. As I did this, I thought my feelings about motherhood might change, but they didn't; I still did not feel a desire to have a child.

I felt unhappy with my career and a lack of deep and lasting purpose in my life. I was great at achieving goals, but reaching them just gave me short-term fulfillment. I saw people I knew find their purpose with the birth of their child. So if I did not want children, what

*Laura Carroll*

would bring me sustained purpose? In my late twenties, I took a job counseling people who had been laid off from their jobs, and not only did I enjoy it, but this work also brought some answers. A few years later, I decided to write a book on what helped my clients (and me) find a deeper sense of purpose in their lives.

When I was writing that book, I felt more fulfilled than I had at any other time in my life to that point. The feminine me had taken the driver's seat in my life, fostering the unfolding of my identity as an artist. I learned that part of a purposeful life for me does involve mothering—mothering the creative process. When writing, I have experienced moments in which I felt the words were conceived from a higher place outside myself. I have become pregnant with information and ideas that I sculpt into a particular form, but ultimately this form takes on a life of its own. I act as a mid-wife of these words—the person who delivers these written creations to the world. I seek to give birth and to nurture through the love, education, and inspiration words can bring. It gives me a deep sense of purpose, and we each have our own pathway to this purpose—through raising a child, caring for nature, or creating books, paintings, or music, to name just a few.

Not wanting children has made it more possible for my husband and me to carve out our own unique lifestyle. At the age of forty, my husband changed careers. After working as a management consultant for over ten years, he began doing environmental work. He has become deeply dedicated to saving the world's ancient forests, and he currently serves as an executive director of an environmental organization. My life does not look nine to five. I primarily consulted to businesses on industrial psychology issues until my mid-thirties, and, since then, have focused less on it and more on my writing. I have orchestrated my life such that I can, as Rainier Maria Rilke put it, "live my questions," while educating and contributing to others through my creative endeavors.

Ten years ago, we bought a vintage cabin on a forested riverfront property in the mountains. We spent nine months a year living in the city and three months in the mountains, before making the cabin our main residence five years ago. We both work from an A-frame adjacent to our home. We love bringing things back to their natural state or essence, and engage ourselves in projects with this theme. One project involved restoring a vintage mountain cabin near us. We get great joy from knowing we can provide guests a peaceful place in nature to rejuvenate and get back to themselves. We enjoy experiencing different cultures and have traveled together to many places in the world. We share the goal of living a life that reflects our love and respect for the earth and all the beings that inhabit it. We also value the power to create our own lifestyle, no matter how conventional or unconventional it may look. Our life is our canvas, and, together, we work toward a life that exemplifies our values in action.

Like us, the couples in this book have carved their own paths in the world as well. My and my husband's backgrounds and lifestyle are also similar to many of theirs in some respects. Like some of them, both of us are oldest children and were the responsible, achiever types growing up. We had to look after our younger siblings, which gave us a taste of what it is like to care for and raise children. In my husband's case, he recollects that his parents expected more of him as the oldest, and he looks back with feelings that very often he did not "get to be a kid" as a child.

As my direction as a writer continued to unfold, my husband and I revisited the topic of a vasectomy. Before we married, I told him I did not want to have children, but he felt sure I would change my mind. My husband said that he not only was committing himself to a life with me, but also to his fulfillment as well as to mine. Although he did not feel drawn to have children, he assumed that I would want them at some point and that we would have them. So if I had wanted children, he would have had them, but once it became clear that I was not going to change my mind, he welcomed my decision. He knew having children would have been a barrier to reaching his personal dreams.

Like a few of the men with whom I talked, my husband also doubts

*Laura Carroll*

that he would make a good father. When he was growing up, his father was impatient, and my husband thinks he would likely be as well. At the same time, because of his desire to be liked, my husband feels he would find it difficult to use strong enough discipline.

Like many of the couples, we don't model traditional gender roles in our marriage. We share domestics and home maintenance work, and I handle the finances. We love our two cats and see them as a wonderful part of our household. We have a mix of friends—some with children, some without. We spend lots of time together. We are involved in our community; love our relationships with our god-children, family, and friend's children; and want to be good role models.

However, more than background or lifestyle, I learned that I am truly not alone in my lack of desire to have children and in my feelings that a child would not fulfill my life. Through these couples, I saw first hand that, although unpopular, a life without children can be just as fulfilling as a life with them. Furthermore, I saw how marriage without parenthood can be as fulfilling as a marriage that chooses parenthood. As I finished this project, my husband and I entered our second decade together, with even more confidence that our marriage would be lifelong.

There are growing numbers of people like the couples in this book who are examples of the many ways to live happily ever after. Today, more people understand that children are one way to leave a legacy and that there are a myriad of ways to live a rich, full life. More and more people see that the choice not to reproduce is a legitimate and worthy choice, and that wanting children is not part of every person's destiny.

# AMY AND BOB

I don't do things because I don't have a reason not to,
but because I *want* to.

-Amy

*A*my and Bob have been married for sixteen years. Amy is from Oregon; Bob grew up in Minnesota and Colorado. They met in a high school cafeteria when they both worked as teachers. Today, Amy teaches junior high school students, and Bob works as the accountant for several small businesses, including an Italian grocery store, and a bicycle repair co-op in their neighborhood.

As I walked up to Amy and Bob's home, I walked through a beautiful flower and vegetable garden in their front yard. We met in their living room on a sunny afternoon, amidst their antique furnishings, plants, and pictures of friends and family. Their cats lounged on the floor in a patch of sun.

~

*How did you decide that you did not want children?*

Amy: I decided when I was in my twenties. There were too many things I wanted to do in my life to afford the years required to raise children. I didn't want to be on my death-bed saying, "I wish I would have . . ." Today, Bob and I have consciously structured our life together so that we work and have enough time to do other things we want to do in our lives.

There were also signals earlier in my life. When I was young, I baby-sat a family over a period of years. In many ways, they were "my kids." Yet, when I watched them, I remember thinking, "only two more hours until it's over." Even then, I could not imagine caring for children on a day-to-day basis.

*Laura Carroll*

Bob: I had a vasectomy about twenty-five years ago. I was in a different relationship at the time, and we decided that overpopulation was the biggest threat to our planet.

During the Vietnam era, my consciousness on environmental issues changed, and I began to see that population exacerbates every environmental problem. Yet, I can't say that population concern is *the* reason I decided not to have children. I felt that having children would have required me to contribute eighteen years of my life to doing something I couldn't see a good reason for doing. It would have taken away options, and required that I be more conventional in certain ways. I would have had to pay more attention to making money and living in a way that was good for the children, rather than in a way that was good for me. I did not want to relinquish this kind of control in my life.

Amy: When Bob and I met, a lot of women my age were having children. I could not imagine having children at that time. I could imagine possibly doing it one day when I felt more settled, and when I had done all the professional things and travel I wanted to do. Yet, deep down, I kept thinking, "I don't want to do this." When Bob told me he had had a vasectomy years ago, I felt free! I no longer had to worry about having or not having children.

*It's widely held that women have children because they are fulfilling a natural biological urge. What do you think about this?*

Amy: I believe we're told to have a biological urge. Society tells us we need to do certain things by a certain time. I see my friends who waited to have children as having more of a "calculated" urge.

Bob: I see it more from a scientist's viewpoint. There is no question a species wants to reproduce itself. In the current stage of human evolution, we are able to separate sex from reproduction, which is a huge change in culture. We can have sex and not reproduce. The urge is the sexual urge, and it's the driving force that ultimately results in reproduction.

*Families of Two*                    ∴ 27 ∽

*Is there anything about you or your background that you think might have influenced you not to want children?*

Bob: I can't imagine having a better family. My parents supported me in whatever I did. They gave me a lot of freedom and independence.

They allowed me to be whatever I wanted to be. I have carried these things into my adult life. I don't want to be controlled, and I want to be able to do what I want to do.

Amy: My grandmother had a big influence on me. I was the youngest of three children, and when my older brother and sister were off doing things, I would often spend time with my grandmother. I think I patterned myself after her. She was tough, independent minded, and loved to cook and garden. In her generation, if you were a woman, you had a child; she and my grandfather had one child, my mom, and that was it. Had she been my age, I bet she would not have chosen to have kids. When my mother got married, my grandmother wanted to know why she *wanted* children!

Given my personality, I think it would be difficult for me to accept that, just because the child is mine, it doesn't mean she/he is going to be like me, think like me, or have the same values I do, even if I expose him/her to them. I could think our child would be like me—someone with a social conscience, who is an environmentalist, and who loves gardening and cats; but, ultimately, I can't control who the child is, or is going to be!

*Do you have any regrets about not having children?*

Amy: Someone once asked me, "What are you going to do when you are seventy and you won't have children there for you?" I thought to myself, "Just because you have children does not mean they are going to take care of you. It doesn't even mean they are going to like you!"

Bob: I have no regrets at all. I *won't* regret not having done the things I wanted to do in my life because of the financial responsibilities associated with children. Amy and I have a great deal of flexibility. We are able to take long periods off of work to travel, and to support ourselves very adequately working less than full-time. I believe it would be almost impossible to have this flexibility if we had children.

*Let's say a couple who is trying to decide whether they want children is asking your advice. What advice would you give to help them make their decision?*

Bob: The most important thing I would tell them is not to do it because they and/or other people think they should. I would encourage them to spend a good amount of time with people who have kids to see what it's really like and how much effort and work parenting involves. People often look at having children as a romantic thing, but it is much more than that! Even the best of kids are demanding—they need a lot of attention, and they should get it. In order to do a good job of parenting, I would tell them it's going to be a hard job. They need to make sure they are willing to take on a very hard job together.

Amy: I would tell them, "Don't just do it if they are thinking, 'Why not?'" I don't do things because I don't have a reason not to, but

*Families of Two* ∴ 29 ∾

because I *want* to. I would advise them to figure out their reason *to* have children. So many people get the job, the car, buy the house, get the dog, and then just—have kids! I would encourage them to come up with a better reason than "it is just what you do." It is so important to look at the many aspects of this decision before making it and to think very hard about it. Many people don't think long and hard enough about such a big decision.

*What impressions do you think others have of you, as a couple that has chosen not to have children?*

Amy: I think it may be harder for my parents to understand me because I am so different than my brother and sister who are raising families. I know they respect my decision not to have children, but I think it challenges them to figure out why I am the way I am.

One of the biggest inaccurate perceptions others have of us is that we are selfish for not having children.

*Do you think you're selfish?*

Amy: I must be, because I decided not to share my life with someone else in this way. I don't think it is bad to be selfish—the word can be a very positive thing. If I am only going to live once, and it means I'm selfish while I live it, so be it!

Bob: I have a different take on this. I don't think we're selfish in a broad sense, because if we were, we wouldn't be doing the community volunteer work we do. We're not materially self-indulgent, like the stereotypical yuppie couple with the sports utility vehicle and the vacation condo at the beach. We don't fit into that cliché at all.

Another aspect of the selfish concept has to do with the many reasons people have children. Some people have them because they want to carry on their genes—what can be more selfish than wanting someone to carry on your genes?! Lots of people also have children because they want something they can mold or vicariously live through.

*Laura Carroll*

For me, selfishness is a matter of orientation. There are different kinds of selfishness. If people tell me I'm selfish for not having kids, are they saying I am supposed to have a child to show I am not selfish? It seems absurd to me.

*How did your love story begin?*

Amy: We were both teaching at the same school, and every day at lunch, Bob, two colleagues, and I would sit in the school cafeteria and solve the problems of the world. At the end of the year, one person in our foursome was leaving, so we arranged a dinner and evening at a local festival. When the other two in our foursome called me to say they couldn't make it, I called Bob to cancel. I hung up, thought a moment, and called him back and said, "I'm ready for dinner; you were ready for dinner a moment ago—why don't we go?" To me, that night was the beginning of things.

Early in our love relationship, we would cuddle on the sofa, talk and talk, fall asleep, wake up, and talk and talk. I have wonderful memories of this time.

*Many couples get married when they're ready to start a family. This wasn't the case for you. Why did you get married?*

Bob: It was a public statement that said I am committed to this person for the rest of my life. I did it so there were no doubts for Amy, or for our families, that I am serious about this commitment.

Amy: When you don't get married, it seems to make the commitment to each other more tenuous.

*What is your life together like?*

Bob: We both work three days a week and have time to do lots of other things. We love to travel. We enjoy cycling; on a recent trip we cycled in New Zealand for three months. We love to read; we are part

of a reading group composed of friends, are currently reading the classics, and loving it.

Giving back to our community is very important to us, and we do quite a bit of volunteer work. We volunteer for the Audubon Society, tutor children, and have adopted a stretch of road to clean near Amy's family cabin in the mountains.

Amy: We are very involved in our local neighborhood association, which works on local park, school, environmental, and political issues. We love to spend time in the garden and play with the cats.

Our concern for the environment is also an integral part of our lifestyle. We work to consciously keep our material needs simple. We recently sold our second car, ride our bikes or the bus whenever we can, recycle, and compost.

*Describe your circle of friends.*

Bob: They run the gamut. Some have children; some don't.

Amy: We have our hobbies, such as reading, cycling, hiking, and playing bridge in common with a number of our friends. With those who are parents, the fact that they have children hasn't affected our

*Laura Carroll*

friendships. With one couple we see a lot of, when their children were small, we knew it would be tougher to see them, so we went to their place to get together.

*How do you handle various aspects of the day-to-day things in marriage, for example, domestics and money management?*

Bob: It's fairly equally divided. Amy does a good share of the cooking, although we share in the preparation much of the time.

Amy: We both love to do the dishes! I do the checkbook, and Bob tracks our investments.

Bob: When we divided up the cleaning, I decided I wanted to take responsibility for the bathroom. It is so typical for women to do the bathroom. I think it is symbolic of gender inequities in our culture.

*What have been your biggest marital challenges?*

Bob: I have had to learn to control my temper. I used to get angry quickly if I felt Amy was trying to control me—to make me do something that was contrary to my basic nature, or do something in a way I did not want to do it. Two things have helped this tendency. Amy is more aware of it now, and I am slower to respond. I've learned to let things sit for a minute, think about it, and, if necessary, cool off.

Amy: We have been working on situations in which we are both angry. So often when we're angry, it's all over from the beginning! So we have worked on not reacting to the heat. We try to figure out what just happened, where we're going, and what we can do differently next time.

I think marital challenges can be compared to going on a long trip with someone. When we have gone on long trips, it was impossible to get along constantly, yet we were stuck with each other, had to work out our differences, and compromise. It's like this in day-to-day married life too.

*Families of Two*

*What are the ingredients to making it work over the long term?*

Amy: It takes a willingness to compromise, and talk to work things out.

Bob: Couples need to respect each other's opinions.

Amy: They also need to have at least one night a week just for the two of them.

Bob: We consciously spend a lot more time than that.

Amy: This is one part of why we decided to have at least one day a week off work. Spending the time together can be as simple as taking a sandwich to the park. I had a good model. My parents had "their" time at the end of the day; the kids knew it was time just for them.

Bob: It's easy to let a relationship atrophy through neglect. Couples have to be consciously committed to keep things strong.

*In your opinion, how does society view the institution of marriage today?*

Bob: I see it evolving, in terms of what is expected in marriage. Society used to consider it an institution for procreation, and often a business relationship. The concept of marrying for love is relatively recent.

Amy: Today, more people accept different kinds of marital relationships, such as same-sex marriages. Couples consciously choosing not to have children is also much more talked about.

Bob: I think society makes divorce too easy. On one hand, it's difficult to know someone very well when you first marry him/her, unless you have had a very long courtship. You've only got one life to live, so you might as well spend it being married to somebody you want to be married to. People should not be forced to stay married if they don't want to be married. On the other hand, it shouldn't be so easy to break the commitment.

Amy: I think we need to teach kids about marriage and let them know that it can look many different ways. We need to do a better job

*Laura Carroll*

of preparing our society's children for real-life issues that they are likely to encounter as adults—and marriage is such an important one.

# BARB AND BILL

It's important to look upon having kids as an option— a
choice, and know that no matter which choice you make,
it will change your life.

-Bill

*B*arb and Bill have been married for twenty-one years. They
both grew up in Oregon. They met at a bus stop and found
out that they lived in the same apartment complex and that their lives
had paralleled in a number of ways. Barb teaches yoga, and Bill has
worked as a neonatalogist for the last seventeen years.

The furniture lined the walls of their living room, leaving an
open space in the center. Barb explained this arrangement was set
up for a yoga class, and asked if I would mind sitting on the floor
during our interview. As we talked, their dog chimed in with a snore
now and then.

~

*How did you decide that you did not want children?*

Barb: The subject came up very early in our relationship. I knew I
did not want to go into a relationship with the expectation of children. I wanted it to be a choice.

I had reservations about having them. I thought having children
would likely threaten my quality of life as an adult woman. When we

met, being a "super mom" who could have it all was a big deal. Being a Type A person at that time, I knew I could be easily sucked into this expectation, but doubted my ability to live up to it. I thought, if I

choose not to do it all, what is the easiest thing not to do? The easier choice was not to have children, given that I needed to financially support myself.

Bill: I grew up assuming I would have kids. Early in our relationship, I remember being interested in having them, but I was very involved with my work. When I met Barb, it became clear to me that if she and I were going to have children, certain criteria would have to be met in order for our relationship to remain intact.

One criterion involved the time I spent with the child. Barb did not want to be a single parent—you can be married and still be a single parent! I needed to be able to spend a fair amount of time with the child. Given my job demands, this just wasn't possible to do in a meaningful way.

Barb: One of my acid tests was if he could promise to be there for the baby's delivery. Given his work demands at the time, he couldn't make this promise.

Bill: I worked twelve-hour days, and was on-call a lot. For a number of years, we said, "Now isn't a good time."

Barb: We kept saying, "At some point things will settle down." When we'd hit that point, we'd find ourselves asking, "Why mess it up?"

Bill: As we re-evaluated having children over a period of years, I became less sure that I wanted them. Having a child now would be a difficult choice for me. I enjoy my lifestyle. I am becoming disentangled from my work, and I like that. To have children at this point would be an encumbrance. The choice not to have them came down to reasons of lifestyle and lingering issues about what kids would mean for our relationship.

Barb: I still have some guilt that I felt less interested than Bill. I wanted it to be a process of ongoing evaluation, but hoped that we'd still come to the same decision not to have them.

*Is there anything about you or your background that you think might have influenced you not to want children?*

Barb: My parents divorced when I was thirteen, and my mother became a single mom. When I was growing up, my mother strongly indoctrinated me not to depend on a man for my money. She was not anti-children, just promoted self-sufficiency. I was not brought up with the formula, "You grow up, get married, and you have kids." I was raised to believe, "You grow up, you get a job, and take care of yourself."

*Laura Carroll*

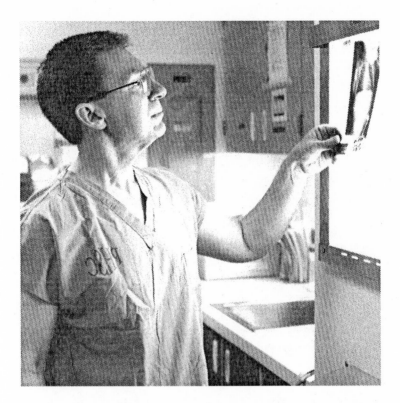

I didn't grow up with the strong expectation of becoming a wife and mother, nor was my identity strongly tied to being a mother. From my early twenties, I began to position myself as a single, professional woman.

*Do you have any regrets about not having children?*

Bill: It's not so much a regret as an issue that will come up. Most people think they will need someone to take care of them when they're older. Barb and I will need to arrange for this kind of support in another way.

I always wanted to carry on a legacy, whatever that means, but it's just a myth we have in our society. Just because we have kids doesn't

460-CARR

mean we'll carry on a great legacy. Just because we have kids also doesn't mean we'll be taken care of someday. They're myths we grew up believing, and a lot of times it works out that way, and a lot of times it doesn't.

Barb: I have no regrets. It was a long process for Bill to come to terms with not having children. When he was having regrets, I used to take him to McDonald's on a Sunday morning, when more children tended to be there. As the kids were bounding off the walls, I would say, "Sure is nice not having kids, isn't it?!"

Bill: When I really admitted it, I didn't particularly like being around kids!

Barb: Just the very, very little babies!

*What are some of the biggest positive aspects of not having children?*

Bill: It has allowed Barb and me time to devote to our relationship. When couples have children, this time has to go on hold awhile. There are probably people who can do both at the same time, but I bet it is very hard.

It has also allowed me to grow personally in ways I never could have, had I had children, because I have had the time to devote to myself. Not having them has also opened up our future in ways that are not available to parents. We have been downsizing and, in two years, plan to put everything in storage and go on an extended cycling trip. This is not the kind of thing people have the opportunity to do when they have kids.

Barb: Not having children has allowed my personal development as well. I have been able to confront my demons without more chaos! There is so much chaos and intrusion on one's well-being, and having children adds another layer of it. I feel I already have my hands full, and it's nice to have the time I do have to process things and keep my sanity. I appreciate not having the distraction of children.

*Laura Carroll*

*Let's say a couple who is trying to decide whether they want children is asking your advice. What advice would you give to help them make their decision?*

Bill: Don't be in a hurry. Work on your relationship with yourself and with your spouse first. For many of us, when we're in our twenties we haven't worked through our issues—we're just getting to a place where we can start to work on them. If the couple decides to have kids, I would encourage them to begin to work through their issues first.

Barb: I would encourage couples to try counseling, either individually or as a couple, and not to go to just one or two sessions, but to commit for a year or so. It is not only an opportunity to talk about such a big decision, but also a chance to deal with things they'll face sooner or later in their lives.

Bill: I would also tell them it's important to look upon having kids as an option—as a choice, and that no matter which choice you make, it will change your life.

*What are others' perceptions of you, as a couple who has consciously chosen not to have children?*

Barb: Surprisingly, women have talked to me more about themselves and their choice to have children. A number of them have told me that if they had it to do over again, they would choose not to have children. It's such a cultural taboo to say this, and I'm so pleased there are more women who are willing to tell the truth about it.

Bill: Society still sends the strong message that you should have children. We may be judged because we don't have them, but we don't get any direct flack about it. As our peers with kids get older, I think they judge us less. As they're dealing with their teenagers, they'll see us cycling in New Zealand!

*Many couples get married when they're ready to start a family. This wasn't the case for you. Why did you get married?*

Barb: We did it largely for practical reasons. The legal reasons to get married just make things more convenient. In part, we got married in order to project a different image when Bill started his fellowship. I think others noted that we were the only couple "living in sin" during his residency.

Bill: There is also this phenomenon in the medical community of "nurses shopping for doc's"—being married made it so much easier for me. It also made a difference to my family.

*What do you do for fun?*

Bill: We cycle quite a bit. Neither of us particularly enjoyed traveling until we started to cycle. We find traveling such a different experience on a bicycle.

Barb: Buying and enjoying our dog has helped us as recovering Type A's.

Bill: Having the dog helps us slow down; we have to come home from work to walk her. Now we take more walks, which is an opportunity to spend more time together.

Barb: We are learning the tango and ballroom dancing—and enjoy it very much!

*How do you handle various aspects of the day-to-day things in marriage, for example, domestics and money management?*

Barb: In the beginning, we tried to have things be "equal," but it wasn't. I am more detail-oriented than Bill on the day-to-day things. Like with the checkbook—I have had to clean up some of his checkbook blunders. Most often, I was the one with the time to go to the bank and straighten things out. It just became easier for me to handle things in the first place.

*Families of Two* ～ 43 ～

Bill: So Barb pays the bills. She does lots of the domestic stuff, and I'm doing more of it. I've learned to cook, which works great for me; coming home and chopping the broccoli helps me shift from being at work to being present at home.

Barb: We have put a lot of effort into positioning these "business of life" things so that we don't get resentful, and feel we're partners in managing it all. We go by the rule, "if 'we' don't cook, 'we' don't eat." I do a lot of the "guy" stuff around the house, like home-improvement projects. We recently re-did the floors, and I took charge of the project.

*Describe your circle of friends.*

Bill: We have just a few friends, with and without kids. Most of the people I know are doctors, and their focus is so different.

Barb: They are often focused on money and opulence. I also think I fell into a bad pattern at an early age of having one best friend. I didn't learn to have multiple friends.

Bill: Now we're running into an awkward situation where we're doing "age-inappropriate" things. I am in my late forties, winding down my career, and most people my age are winding their careers up. My partners don't want to hear about our lifestyle or the trip.

Barb: It can threaten people who are doing certain things with their money and careers to hear you can live life in another way. We have received two very different reactions from people when we've told them we are going on the bike trip. One is, "You shouldn't do it," either because it's not safe, or because we have responsibilities. The other is, "Don't wait to go."

Bill: We hope plugging more into the cycling community will help us make new friends.

*Many couples talk about creating something together. Have you had similar feelings?*

Bill: I struggle with this idea because I feel that I'd like to create

*Laura Carroll*

something that's lasting, and that has permanence. Yet, I believe that you can't create anything that's permanent. Why create something grand, when even the grandest things come to nothing? With this belief, there is nothing to take to the relationship to create something. I focus my creation on day-to-day things, like providing my patients with good care.

Barb: I agree. My creation relates to how my life can give to people. Through teaching yoga, I realize I am a role model on some level for how to live differently in the world. We have been downsizing, learning to live more simply, choosing to do less, and for Type A's, this can model what another life can look like.

People have given to us in this way. One time we were on the coast and ran into cyclists. We talked to them, and they don't know it, but it's because of them that we're going to quit our jobs and go out on the road for a year. We never know how we are affecting other people!

I feel modeling a healthy relationship also gives to the world. It gives courage to people who aren't in a healthy relationship to do something about it. We can serve as an indirect, confrontive, yet positive force that helps people question the way they are living their lives.

*What have been your biggest marital challenges?*

Barb: When I met Bill, he was one person, and right after we married, when he started his internship and residency, he "went away." I kept waiting for the person I met to come back.

Bill: I lived a horrible lifestyle during my residency. For a long time, I blocked everything else out of my life and "numbed out" to survive. The field of medicine is set up so that this horrible lifestyle continues when a doctor goes into practice.

Barb: His relationship with his work became an issue early in our relationship. At first I said, "It'll get better when his internship is over." Then I said, "When his residency is over . . ."; then, "When his fellowship is over . . ."; and then, "When his practice . . ."

We waited a long time for things to get better, and I felt I had been carrying the pain for the relationship. For too long, I talked myself into why I should wait. I finally told Bill it just wasn't working, and asked that we get into counseling together.

Bill: One of the biggest things I needed to look at was my relationship with my work. While counseling has had a profound impact on our relationship, it has helped me take a hard look at why I chose my profession and why I worked as much as I did. I've gotten a much better understanding of myself.

*What are the ingredients to making it work over the long term?*

Barb: Mutual trust and respect.

Bill: I think couples need more than this. Couples have to be able to communicate. If they can't communicate, they can't get through the rough spots.

Couples also have to be able to keep coming back to recurring issues until they are resolved. An important attitude to hold during these times is, "the reason the other person is upset is a reason I need to understand." This attitude helps prevent resentment levels from getting too high. If resentment gets high, it can be very destructive.

*In your opinion, how does society view the institution of marriage today?*

Bill: Lots of subgroups of society may disagree, but society projects the image that marriage is still very important.

Barb: Unlike what society may say, I don't think going from unmarried to married said a whole lot about our relationship. We kept the ceremony simple with a Justice-of-the-Peace in my parents' living room. Marriage just simplified things, and wasn't a big deal.

Bill: Marriage or no marriage, the big deal is Barb. I am so glad I have Barb. Having her as my life companion is so important to me.

*Laura Carroll*

*Families of Two*  ~ 47 ~

# VICKI AND NATHAN

We have given birth to many things in our marriage; we
just haven't given birth to children.

-Vicki

*V*icki and Nathan have been married for fourteen years. Vicki
grew up in Los Angeles, and Nathan is from San Diego. They
met through a mutual friend.

Vicki is a singer and theater actor. Nathan is a computer scientist.
I met with them in the living room of their charming home on a hot,
summer night. Their cat looked on, purring.

~

*What are the biggest reasons you decided not to have children?*

Vicki: I knew early in my life that I did not want children. A big
reason has to do with my work. Even as a young child, I knew I had a
passion for singing and acting. I love my work, and I love *to* work. I
work all the time. I knew early on that this was not a very good way to be
a parent.

Nathan: I didn't so much decide not to have kids, as not to decide
to have kids. I don't seem to have inherited a parenting gene; I haven't
had the urge to do it. My decision not to have children really happened when I hooked up with someone who had decided not to.

I also know that I have somewhat of a low threshold for overload. I ran across a book called *The Highly Sensitive Person*, and it talks about people who seem to have their input circuits stuck on high—people

who are easily over-stimulated or who can easily go on stimulation overload. There are many people like this, and it's not the sort of thing we hear much about. It is just the way some people are wired. This book gave me a good description of my interaction with today's high-output world.

When I see parents with children, it strikes me how much input they have to be able to take. For me, it would make parenting very rough. It looks like an awfully hard job, harder than any job I've ever done.

*It's widely held that women have children because they are fulfilling a natural biological urge. What do you think about this?*

Vicki: I know it exists, but for some women, the urge may come more from the "*why don't you* have kids" pressure than from a true urge.

Nathan: Evolution has programmed us to perpetuate the species, from the pleasures of sex, to the nurturing instinct, to the mysteries of love. I'm not convinced there's a biological urge to be a parent, but there are enough other urges to push most people in that direction.

Vicki: I'm only forty-four, and the onset of menopause began three years ago. When it first started, I remember thinking my "time is up" and feeling a brief twinge inside. When Nathan got a vasectomy, I had another little twinge.

*What was the twinge saying?*

Vicki: That a choice was being taken away.

Nathan: We were cutting off an option that we, so far, had waited to exercise, and now we can't. Nobody likes to be deprived of choice, even if they happily choose the same thing—the same job, the same marriage, the same life—every day. It's that power to choose that makes humans unique.

Vicki: And for me, I have to be able to say "yes" before I can say "no," and vice versa. No longer having the choice was what those twinges were about, not the fact that I would no longer be able to have a family.

*Is there anything about you or your background that you think might have influenced you not to want children?*

Nathan: I have always been independent, sought a lot of solitude, and tended to get into things to the point of obsession. When I was nine years old, my dad noticed I was spending a good deal of time in my room, studying the solar system. It fascinated me; I delved into books, charts, and pictures. I told him it was for a school project. My dad began to think I was spending an incredible amount of time on it, and he asked me if it were really for a school project. I told him the truth—I was studying it just because it had caught my interest. When my dad asked me why I told him it was for a school project, I said, "Because I thought I'd get into trouble!" I still work this way. I get deeply into things. I am sort of a pathological engineer.

*Laura Carroll*

Vicki: I think my parental background influenced me. Growing up, I got the feeling that my mother liked the idea of children better than actual children. She did not typify the "stay-at-home" mom. She did what was open to women in the fifties. She worked as a dental assistant for almost fifty years.

She abdicated to the mother role but also wanted a lot of control. She scheduled her children's births, and had C-sections on her day off. This gives you an indication of what my mother was like. I am like her in this respect: efficient and in control.

My father worked as an engineer. At home, I remember him as absent and uninvolved. My memory pictures him as a retreating figure—someone who is turning his back from me as he walks away. I come from an Italian family, so there was a lot of talking and conflict, but I wouldn't describe the family feeling as warm and connected.

When I was sixteen, my parents divorced. Before then, my mother, brother, and I had a common enemy in my father. When he was gone, all hell broke loose. The family unit dissolved. In many ways, my brother and I were on our own. Being the oldest, I often took charge and was the responsible one.

*Let's say a couple who is trying to decide whether they want children is asking your advice. What advice would you give to help them make their decision?*

Nathan: I would encourage them not to have children until they know it is something they truly want and feel ready to do. Many people become parents not so much because they decide to, but because they don't decide not to. Or it's something they just do because it's expected of them. These are the wrong reasons to become a parent.

Vicki: From the point of view of someone who experienced less than wonderful parenting, I would encourage them to become hyperaware of the responsibility that comes with parenting. It's not so much the daily responsibilities, as the ultimate responsibility for the shape of somebody's life. This is a <u>huge</u> thing. People need to be ready to take on this kind of responsibility, or their children will ultimately suffer, as I well know.

*Laura Carroll*

*What perceptions do you think other people have of you, as a couple that has chosen not to have children?*

Vicki: Sometimes, I think people think we're lucky.

Nathan: And I think others feel sorry for us, for not knowing the pleasures of parenting. I admit that we can't begin to understand the rewards of having children.

Vicki: A friend said to me years ago, "You are parenting people's creativity." Teaching has clearly played the parenting role in my life. Over the years, I have taught ages from seven to seventy.

I think people often believe that people who choose not to have kids don't like kids. It's not true for me. One former student feels like an adopted daughter to me. I also have quite an affinity for high school kids. I love their energy, passion, and new awareness of the world.

*Based on your experience, what are society's assumptions or misconceptions about married couples who consciously choose not to parent?*

Vicki: I think others easily see childless couples as selfish.

*Is it true?*

Vicki: For me, yes—I think an artist's life can look very self-indulgent.

Nathan: By making the decision not to have children, we are foregoing some of the sacrifices people make when they have kids, like financial and time sacrifices.

*Does choosing not to sacrifice these things equate to selfishness?*

Nathan: It can, yet choosing these sacrifices can also come from a selfish place. Sometimes, people have children for selfish reasons too.

Vicki: I sacrificed a lot of my childhood to my parents, a couple of human beings who in many ways were incapable of being in control of

my life. If someone accused me of being selfish because I am not making the sacrifices associated with having children, I would tell them I made my sacrifices early on in my life. Many people don't make sacrifices until they're older; I made mine right away. I didn't begin to experience life from a clear, accepting place until I was in my thirties.

Nathan: We have avoided certain sacrifices, but in the eyes of people who believe that having kids brings one of the great joys in life, we have experienced sacrifices. Some parents may not see us as selfish, but as lacking, or deserving of pity.

Twenty to forty years from now, we will sacrifice not having adult children to love and appreciate. We will not have someone to help us in our old age if we need it, or to come to our funerals.

*Laura Carroll*

*Will you regret this?*

Nathan: I don't know. Ultimately, what will my legacy be? These great engineering projects? I am not sure how much of a legacy that leaves the world. Perhaps, the people I have touched and affected throughout my life constitute the greater legacy.

Vicki: The connection we make with people, that certain energy source in a relationship—I see this as the legacy. It gives to others, and feeds out into the community. I'm not hooked into legacy through family because I've experienced considerable pain in this area of my life. I think of legacy in terms of the larger community.

*Do you consider yourselves part of the mainstream?*

Vicki: We're not mainstream, because we don't have kids. We aren't mainstream in the sense that we utterly love our work. Neither one of us could imagine doing anything else.

In another way we are mainstream—we have the house, and the car. Nathan makes good money, and it allows us to live in a nice place, but our life does not revolve around the trappings. Sometimes, I feel guilty, as an artist, because I want to contribute more financially. Then I think, how does one judge worth? It means so much more than how much money a person can put in the bank. I wouldn't say this perspective fits into the mainstream view of worth.

When I met Nathan, I expected him to run far and fast when I told him I was a singer. Instead, he thought it was great. The way I see it, by Nathan supporting us, he is supporting the arts. He gives so much more than financial support; he encourages and supports me in every way.

Nathan: Maybe I stray from the mainstream by not having had the maturing experience of parenthood. Sometimes, I feel like I put off childhood until I was grown up.

Vicki: This rings true for me too. My work demands that I keep many aspects of the kid in me.

*How did your love story begin?*

Vicki: Nathan and I hit it off right away!

Nathan: I came to visit Vicki's roommate one weekend, and she introduced us. The next day we went flying in a small plane and had a great time.

Vicki: He came back the following Friday, and . . .

Nathan: . . . we did not get much sleep that night!

Vicki: That was the beginning of things. We got married a year later, to the day.

*What kind of time do you spend together?*

Vicki: We try to always have breakfast and dinner together, unless I have a rehearsal or show. We spend many evenings at home, each buried in our work. On the weekends, we spend lots of time together.

Nathan: I read a study that said the average number of minutes couples spend together is twenty minutes a day! We spend much more time than that.

Vicki: We have a garden, and talk a lot about food. We both read quite a bit, and we talk about what we're reading, whether it be a newspaper article or a book.

Nathan: Because I have a background in theater, we have the performing arts in common.

*How do you handle the practical aspects of marriage, for example, domestics and money management?*

Nathan: I have the main breadwinner's job, and for a while, we associated it with the responsibility of bill paying, but Vicki is just better with these kinds of details. The day I finally dropped the checkbook on her desk, things became much more organized.

Vicki: I am good at the day-to-day details, and Nathan is good at big

*Laura Carroll*

picture stuff, like projecting our finances over time and managing our investments. We both cook, and I do the domestics.

*What is your circle of friends like?*

Nathan: In the past twenty years, many of our friends have had children. A social gap existed between us and them because we didn't have one big topic of conversation in common.

Vicki: We noticed for a period of years that we'd be close to people, they would have children, and we would never see them again.

Nathan: We're now reaching an age where a lot of our friends' kids are graduating from high school, and they are becoming more available.

Vicki: Like me, my best friend has no children. Most of my other friends include artists and single women who are younger than me. I find people my own age can sometimes be a bit stodgy!

*Many couples talk about creating something together. Have you had similar feelings?*

Nathan: Several years ago, we started a theater company called Open Heart Theatre. Running Open Heart required us to support each other and maintain the ability to do an infinite amount of work to bring art into the world. Many people benefited from what we did at Open Heart.

Vicki: We were more than a marriage—we were an industry! We were, and are, such a great team. I can't imagine a better match for me. We have given birth to a lot of things in our marriage; we just haven't given birth to children.

*What have been your biggest marital challenges?*

Vicki: About eight years into our marriage, we individually had very busy lives. Nathan was attending graduate school, working full-time, and rehearsing for a show. I was teaching and doing show after show. We weren't seeing much of each other, and I eventually became unsure about wanting to be married. It was then that we started addressing what wasn't working in our marriage.

*What was most important to making it through?*

Nathan: Even though we both had lots going on, we made time to make our marriage the most important priority.

Vicki: I read the book, *Getting the Love You Want,* and it helped us start the dialogue.

Nathan: We began to understand the difference in our communication styles. Learning how to communicate better with each other helped us break through what wasn't good in our marriage.

*In your experience, what are the ingredients to keeping a marriage alive?*

Vicki: Spend time together. Talk about things, no matter how difficult. It also really makes a difference to give your partner what she/he wants. In our period of struggle, I realized it's not so much about getting what *I* want *from* the relationship, as it is about finding what I can *give to* Nathan and the relationship. Also, it's not his job to make me happy in life; it's my own responsibility.

Nathan: When things get rough, it can be so easy to turn your back on the marriage; it's the hardest thing in the world to turn around and face it, but I think one needs to be willing to do this for a marriage to last.

*How does society see the institution of marriage today?*

Nathan: It depends on who is talking. It seems to me that most speakers bemoaning the state of marriage have a political agenda and a need to force their definition of family on everyone else. They helped drive the Religious Right a few years ago.

*Laura Carroll*

Vicki: Creating the "right" marriage box excludes a whole world of couples and families. Today, marriage and family look many different ways, like same-sex marriages and blended families. The primary relationships in one's life often define family just as much as blood relationships do. I have friends that are more "family" to me than my real family.

However, in today's society, people have many fears, economic fears in particular. For many people, fitting into the "right" structure eases their fears, and they feel safer. Specifically, they feel safer if they can say, "We have the right marriage, job, kids, house, and cars; we go to church, and worship the right God." How can they be right and others also be right? I think it's hard for our society to embrace the idea that I can be right, and that others can be right too.

Nathan: Maybe it's the Puritan component of America's background finally reasserting itself. Is the Puritan gene in the American body politic still very much alive?

Vicki: How people's choices affect the way we view and accept each other. It relates to so much more than the choice not to have children; it ultimately reflects the state of our world.

*Families of Two*

# FREDI AND CARLOS

We got out of that "box" that insists having kids is the only
way you can have real impact.

-Fredi

*F*redi and Carlos have been married for twenty-four years.
They grew up in San Diego, California. They lived in the
same neighborhood and met when they were teenagers. Their
romance began about two years after Carlos graduated from high
school when they saw each other at a party.

Fredi teaches university communications courses, and is completing her doctoral degree in cultural studies. Carlos has college degrees in architectural technology and urban studies, and is a
professional in affordable housing development and urban
revitalization. We met in their living room on a spring evening.

~

*How did you decide that you did not want children?*

Fredi: In the seventies, when I was about thirteen, I read my first
feminist book, *Memoirs of a Prom Queen*. Then I read Simon DeBeauvier,
and her line, "women who have children will never be free" hit me
like a ton of bricks. I realized having children would compromise my

choices in life and prevent me from living to my potential. Before we got married, I made it very clear to Carlos that I did not want children.

Carlos: It was all right with me. Not having children aligned with my environmental attitudes. We grew up with the influence of the sixties and seventies, and I was aware of how the population explosion was affecting our urban and natural environments.

Even so, when we got married, I wanted children more than Fredi did. As time passed, the lines on the chart crossed for us. My desires have reduced, and on occasion Fredi has brought up the idea of adoption.

Fredi: There are so many kids that need love. I still don't want a baby, but once in awhile I have this fleeting thought that parenthood would be interesting. Then I think of my work—and my life takes over!

*Is there anything about you or your background that you think might have influenced you not to want children?*

Fredi: I was not raised to be a wife and mother. I have one sister, and no brothers. If my father would have had a son, my parents may have been more traditional with me. They raised me to be strong and vocal, to fight for my rights, and to not let anyone take advantage of me.

I am fiercely independent and have always valued my freedom. My grandmother was a soldier in the Mexican revolution, and my father's parents came to the United States during the revolution. Generally speaking, Mexican-Americans are very conservative people and don't like to make waves, but my father broke away, was a leftist, and became involved in the Chicano movement. He was a union man. My parents talked about social justice issues and fought for the underdog. They had forums at our house and encouraged me to participate.

My father was also the head of the house. I knew early in my life that I didn't want to be a traditional, subservient wife.

Carlos: I was the second child, and the first son in a large family. I was a serious kid and became aware of political, social, and environmental issues at a young age. My parents loved us, and sometimes struggled to provide the material things that kids need. I did not want to feel these kinds of pressures.

　　　　　*Laura Carroll*

*Do you have any regrets about not having children?*

Carlos: I have thought about what it would have been like to have a child. Once I was riding on my mountain bike with a young man in his early twenties, and I thought to myself, "I could have a kid this age! And we could be out biking right now." Then I thought, "If I had a

child tomorrow and rode with him/her at the age of twenty, I'd be in my sixties!"

Fredi: Sometimes, I think about having children because soon it is not going to be a choice anymore. I am in my early forties, and my biological clock has ticked out. When I go through menopause, I don't know if I will have real moments of regret.

Others have expressed regrets to me, but about *having* children. I can't tell you how many people have said to me, "Fredi, don't do it," because of their own feelings of regret. This has stuck with me.

*What has been toughest about not having children?*

Fredi: I find more things annoying than tough. It annoys me that people often assume I am infertile. People I have just met have also asked me why I don't have children. When I was younger, if people I didn't know asked me this, I'd say, "What color of underwear do you have on?" to point out it's a very private thing to ask.

Carlos: It is frustrating to try to educate people so that they understand that I consciously chose not to have children. No matter what I tell them, they often have difficulties understanding that it is a personal choice.

*Let's say a couple who is trying to decide whether they want children is asking your advice. What advice would you give them to help them make their decision?*

Carlos: I'd tell them what I have found beneficial about not having children. Fredi and I have enjoyed full adult lives. Children haven't compromised our choices. Call it greed or selfishness, but I have been able to pursue things I would not have been able to if I would have had children.

Many people say they'll have their children early, raise them, and then do the kinds of things Fredi and I have done. I don't think it's possible. I wouldn't want to do the things I did in my twenties when I'm in my forties. Even if I did, it wouldn't be the same experience. Going to Europe in my twenties would be very different than going in my forties.

*Laura Carroll*

Fredi: In the interpersonal communications courses I teach, we talk about family. Students ask me about having children, and when I share my choice with them, I get mixed reactions. Some students get upset. I tell them it's my choice, and it is my life. I say having children is a wonderful thing to do, but make sure it's what *you* want to do, that it will satisfy a need in you, not just a need in your parents or spouse. Don't do it just because it's a social or cultural imperative. This is especially important with my female students of color.

Carlos: I would tell Mexican-American men that if they decide not to have children, other men of the culture may think of them as being "less" than most men. They may question them about whether they are good providers, or whether they are good sexually. I have also heard many men of the culture say, "He's a fag; he doesn't have kids." They think not having children means that you must not like to have sex with a woman; otherwise, you'd have children!

One way that traditional Mexican culture measures machismo is by the number of children a man has. You are virile, you are potent, because you have children. This is a fallacy. Even so, if Mexican-American men choose not to have kids, they'll have to be strong enough not to let others get the best of them, because questions and accusations will be common. I'd advise them to be prepared because the culture will come at them, and they won't always be surrounded by people who understand or accept their choice.

*What impressions do you think others have of you, as a couple that has chosen not to have children?*

Fredi: I think some members of our families feel sorry for us.

Carlos: They probably think Fredi influenced me a lot, and it wasn't so much my choice as it was hers. Some family members most likely see us as unfulfilled, in part because we don't have children. I think it's a lot easier for them to see Fredi as the selfish one, or to blame her for things that don't fit their model of how I should be as a male, married adult.

On selfishness—in some cultures, as I mentioned, men are measured by the number of children they have. Isn't this a selfish reason to have children? It isn't necessarily because they love children or want to give to a child; it's because they need to be considered a man in the culture. I'm a dad, period. That's all that matters.

Fredi: Many Mexican-Americans we know think there must be something wrong with us because we don't fit their mold. Part of the mold has to do with class. Most of our family is working class; Carlos and I are too, but have broken out of the mold of what it looks like to be working class in our culture.

For example, I don't fit the traditional wife mold. I am a very strong woman. It is not to say women in my culture are not strong—

they are strong!—but even in my generation many Mexican-American women were raised to be wives and mothers, and to be subservient to their husbands.

Some people have looked at my choices and lifestyle, and accused me of trying to be "white," of trying to be something I am not. They also have had the misconception that we have a lot of money.

Sometimes, the misconceptions influence people's feelings. I have felt resentment from some women with children. Sometimes, I think I am a mirror for them. Maybe they see a reflection of the choices they wish they would have made, or who they could have become. Their unacknowledged regret can get projected onto me in the form of resentment.

Carlos: People with children have also told us we're superficial. It might be easy not to give us any kind of depth, because if they did, it might make them think, "I didn't have to have kids?"

Fredi: They might be forced to interrogate their choices more closely.

*Were you ever pressured to have children?*

Carlos: When my brothers and sisters had kids, it relieved the pressure my family tried to put on me.

Fredi: My father has no problem with my not having children. Now that my mother is the only one without grandchildren, every once in awhile, she lets it slip out how great she thinks it would be.

I think Carlos' family would die of happiness if we had kids, but I think they have made peace with our decision.

*What do you see as your role in molding the next generation of children?*

Carlos: Through me, I want my nieces and nephews to see they have a choice of how to live their lives. They don't have to follow the same old traditions. It's all right to live another type of life.

I speak to classes in schools and help students of lower socioeconomic backgrounds see it's OK to pursue professional goals,

*Families of Two*

and to do things that are different from what they may normally see in their lives.

Professionally, we both recognize our roles in molding the next generation of children. Fredi is a university instructor. I am responsible for the development of affordable housing and transitional housing opportunities for families with children. We take our roles quite seriously.

Fredi: Our nieces and nephews are very important to us. We want to help them expand their horizons and perspectives about the world.

*How did your love story begin?*

Fredi: I went to a party with Carlos' cousin. Carlos was there, and the rest is history. We got married young; I was nineteen, and Carlos was twenty-one.

Carlos: We had no idea how much we didn't have, in terms of material support. We didn't have much money between us. Fredi was working at a clerk job, and I was working part-time on boats and going to school.

*Do you believe there is a purpose in the two of you coming together?*

Carlos: Fate brought us together. Right now, I am supporting Fredi's educational pursuits. She will make a big mark somewhere.

Fredi: I love to teach. I feel fortunate that I discovered my calling at this point in my life and that I have a life partner who celebrates my choices.

Carlos: There is a bigger plan for us all. I don't know what mine is yet. In the meantime, my professional and community work impacts people's lives. Most of those I help will never know my name.

Fredi: We got out of that "box" that insists having kids is the only way you can have real impact. Being together has allowed each of us to make an impact in our own ways. Every life touches other lives in ways we

*Laura Carroll*

can't ever know or begin to understand. I think our purpose is to touch people in those ways. Teaching gives me an opportunity to do this.

*What is your life together like?*

Carlos: We both work during the week and have dinner together most evenings. We socialize with friends and family, travel, and spend a lot of personal time doing community activism work.

Fredi: Our community work is very important to us. We are active in Latino organizations, and involve ourselves in activities that educate and inspire people in our community to become politically active.

I am also involved with a group that supports indigenous women in Chiapas. I studied the Zapatista National Liberation Army's use of the Internet as a grass-roots tool for cultural emancipation for my thesis. I received a fellowship for further study, spent time in Chiapas, and saw the situation first-hand. I continue to strongly support this movement.

*Tell me about your circle of friends.*

Carlos: We met most of our current friends through work and community activities. They reinforce our childless choice. Most of our friends are non-traditional. We have a lot of friends who are gay. We have a strong connection to the gay community because they, too, exist outside the norm. A number of friends are straight, single adults. There are childless couples too.

Fredi: We've had friendships with more traditional couples, but most often, it just never worked out. Once they started to have a family, we would get together less and less.

*How do you handle various aspects of the day-to-day things in marriage, for example, domestics and money management?*

Carlos: Before we got married, Fredi told me she didn't cook, and

*Families of Two*

this is still the case. I don't cook much either, so we eat out a lot, which I enjoy!

Fredi: Over the course of our marriage, we've hired several cleaning people. When I go "underground," as I call it, and get immersed in my academic work, Carlos does more than his fair share of things.

*What have been your biggest marital challenges?*

Carlos: I believe in a filing system, and Fredi believes in a piling system!

Fredi: Carlos' environment is important to him. He is very visually attuned. I have a different style; I am a pile woman! We each have had to give a little to work it out. He has become more patient when I am into something and have stacks of books around me. I have to step outside of myself and realize it's driving him nuts. We are much better at working it out now than even a year ago. It is the major difference between us.

*In your experience, what are the ingredients that have made your marriage work?*

Fredi: So many things don't have to be explained. We come from the same culture and socioeconomic background. Our families grew up in the same neighborhood and know each other. We instantly understand the little nuances that wouldn't make sense to somebody from a different culture or ethnicity.

Carlos: We have the same Catholic upbringing. We understand the church and can get mad at it for the same things.

Fredi: Our religious practice also has a strong indigenous influence. It is not the same type of Roman Catholicism that many Anglos practice. Our families talk openly about ghosts and experiences in the spirit world.

Carlos: We have the same politics. That's a biggie. We are not looking for a lot of material wealth in life. We want more of an equal

*Laura Carroll*

level of participation in our relationship, rather than one person being the dominant one. Not having children has allowed us to pursue our interests and grow.

Fredi: Because of this, there is always something new in our life together. It keeps it interesting and less routine.

*What does being married mean to you?*

Fredi: Getting married says this relationship is not a "fly by night" thing, and we are committed to making it work.

Carlos: Even as young, immature, and inexperienced as we were when we got married, we knew it was about commitment. We had strong role models around us. Our parents and married relatives

around us. Our parents and married relatives showed us that marriage is serious and that it's about staying committed to each other, no matter what.

# CAROL AND ROBERT

Because we weren't feeding and clothing children,
paying babysitters, and saving for college,
we have been able to enjoy each other and our life
together in so many ways.

-Carol

*C*arol and Robert have been married for thirty-six years. Robert was raised just north of New York City, and Carol grew up in New Jersey. Robert has worked as a tax attorney for over thirty years. They met when Robert did Carol's tax return. She has had a career in health care, and currently consults to educational agencies on health careers planning. We met on a spring afternoon, in the conference room of Robert's forty-third floor office.

~

*How did you decide that you did not want children?*

Carol: I have never been exactly keen on the idea of becoming a parent, and have never really liked little children When I was 21, I had a fairly serious illness that resulted in my not being able to conceive. I know it sounds strange, but the only thing that bothered me about it was telling my parents.

We went into the marriage knowing we could choose to adopt, but adoption never got past "maybe next year." Our decision not to adopt gradually evolved over the first twenty years of our marriage.

Robert: Because it required a very conscious decision for us to have a child, we really had to want it before we did it. We were probably wise not to have them because I honestly have never really liked children—if I didn't like them, what kind of parent would I be?

Yet before we were married, initially I was disturbed when Carol told me she couldn't have children. I weighed the pluses and minuses, and felt it was a small minus compared to many pluses. I felt we might adopt at some point. Over time, these feelings faded away.

We were enjoying our life together. When adoption came up, I think we talked about it because we thought it was something we were supposed to do—everybody had children then.

Carol: I don't think I would have been a good parent. I have a nasty temper that I keep under control most of the time. I can be patient, but in small doses, and children aren't in small doses. They are not something you can give back when you are tired of them. I am great with children, but twenty-four hours a day, seven days a week for twenty years? I don't think so. Parenting was not something I could ever see myself doing on a daily basis.

*It's widely held that women have children because they are fulfilling a natural biological urge. What do you think about this?*

Carol: I think it's more about social pressure. I was young when I knew I did not want to be a parent. It never occurred to me to put myself through what I see so many women put themselves through to conceive their "own" child. There are so many children who need good parents. Reproduction at this point in time is a highly selfish thing, because of how many people are already here, but at the same time, I recognize there is human desire to replicate oneself, and to experience a sense of immortality by leaving something of one's self behind.

*Is there anything about you or your background that you think might have influenced you not to want children?*

Robert: I am an only child and was never around children growing up. I have never really felt comfortable with them.

Carol: My father went away to Pearl Harbor when I was thirteen months old. He was missing from my life until I was three. My grandmother worked one shift in the Navy Yard, and my mother another, and they traded off taking care of me. There weren't children to play with in our neighborhood, so I became more comfortable being around adults.

*Laura Carroll*

I didn't like being a child. I was one of those "adult" children. I was the oldest and the responsible one.

I am not sure my mother or my father liked being parents. I could tell they weren't really sure what to do with my younger sister and me. If they had a choice, I don't think they would have had children.

*Do you have or think you will have any regrets about not having children?*

Carol: Maybe thirty seconds on Christmas Eve when I see those Hallmark cards!

Robert: I suppose 1% of me will have a bit of regret. When I balance it with all that is involved in raising a child, 99% of me has no regrets. The 1% fantasizes that when I am ninety, I could have had a son who became a Supreme Court justice!

*Were you ever pressured to have children?*

Carol: There was a lot of social pressure to have children years go.

Robert: The post-war mentality of the 1950's, the time of Doris Day and Ozzie and Harriet, created big social pressures. Women went to college for their "MRS." degree, as they say, got married, and had children. This was the norm in our country at the time.

Carol: Then in the early sixties, birth control became available, and for the first time, women actually had a certain amount of say over their reproductive process, but pressures still exist today. I remember talking to a young first generation American woman at my gym. Her parents are Croatian. She was married to a Croatian man. They had only been married two years, and they were getting serious pressure to have children. That is the culture.

Robert: In my situation, if Mother had lived long enough, she would have pressured us.

Carol: I am sure of it.

Robert: But she died two weeks after our first anniversary. On my father's side, one sister had kids, but the two others did not, so they could understand. My mother had a brother and a sister who never married. Another brother had a child later in life. So there was no "big" family, thus, less pressure.

Carol: My family didn't pressure us. Maybe they didn't because they weren't into parenting themselves. I think they were just grateful

*Laura Carroll*

that I was married—I was twenty-three when I got married, and that was old in those days!

*What has been toughest about not having children?*

Carol: Between the two of us, we essentially have no family and won't as we get older. I am grateful for good, loyal friends.

Robert: We have very specific instructions regarding our funeral arrangements and the like, because there isn't family to do it.

*What are the biggest positives about not having children?*

Robert: We can do what we want—it's that simple!

Carol: We love to travel and have traveled throughout our marriage. Because we weren't feeding and clothing children, paying babysitters, and saving for college, we have been able to enjoy each other and our life together in so many ways.

*Let's say a couple who is trying to decide whether they want children is asking your advice. What advice would you give to help them make their decision?*

Carol: I'd tell them not to have children to make their spouse happy, their mother happy, their mother-in-law happy, and their family happy, or to climb the corporate ladder. Have them for one reason—because the two of you want them. As far as being ambivalent, even if they decide not to have children today, that doesn't mean they can't change their minds tomorrow.

Robert: But once they have them, they can't undo it.

*What impressions do you think others have of you, as a couple that has chosen not to have children?*

Robert: The impressions depend on the people, and where they come from. For example, if they come from a conventional Italian, Catholic family, maybe they feel there's something wrong because we don't have children.

Carol: Years ago, it often felt awkward, because being childless then was a very unusual thing. We commonly heard, "What's wrong with who?" from others, but I don't think people have thought any

*Laura Carroll*

less of me. Some people see us as a "special" case. We are not only childless, but also in a mixed religious marriage. Others see us as unique. They don't judge us or perceive us within the same framework as they do their other friends. They see us a bit like exotic birds.

Maybe some people have felt sorry for us because we don't have what they think is the most wonderful thing in the world. Sometimes, I have felt that others think I can't relate to them, since I can only intellectually understand being the mother of a child. Some people may also see us as irresponsible in some ways because we don't have the responsibilities that go with parenting. We just have different responsibilities.

In general, I think society sees childless people as selfish, but truthfully, when I see some couples with children, I often think they are the ones who are the most selfish. I have seen couples walking with their dogs on one leash, and a toddler on another! This is selfish. I recognize the need for nannies and childcare when both people are working—at the same time, the nanny may be the only one who really knows the child. Too often, people see children as an extension of themselves, or as another "trophy" that adds to their whole image.

Robert: There was a time when, in so-called "corporate America," men had to be married and have a family. It fit the image of being a stable, responsible person. Marital and parental status still factor into the "corporate" image, but less so these days. Today, both men and women are judged more by who they are.

Carol: I wish more people have the impression I do of couples who decide not to have children. Maybe it comes from a white, upper-middle-class, urban perspective, but all it says to me is that a couple has given something serious thought, and found for their own reasons that it's better for them not to have children. That's all.

*How do you see yourselves as different from people who have children?*

Carol: We are less religious, and have a broader tolerance for mixed religious marriages and mixed racial marriages. On the whole, religious identity seems to become more of an issue when people have children.

Robert: That's because parents often feel they have to give their children religious identification and structure. They see it as an obligation that goes with parenting.

*What do you see as your role in molding the next generation of children?*

Carol: We believe in helping young people reach their academic goals, and this gives us great satisfaction. We are contributing directly to the college education of a widowed friend's daughter, and fund scholarships at New York University's School of Law, and the Stern School of Business at NYU, as well as Cornell's Johnson Graduate School of Management, our alma maters.

*Tell me about how your love story began.*

Carol: After he did my tax return, Robert asked me out. We had our first date on the thirtieth of June, and we were engaged by the seventeenth of July!

Robert: We were married on the twenty-third of October that same year.

Carol: We entered into a mixed religious marriage in a time when this was very rare. Robert was Jewish, and I was Catholic. It was hard to find someone to marry us.

Robert: Aside from being in love with her, right away I felt Carol was someone I could live with. That is what marriage is. I was thirty-one, and Carol may have been only twenty-three, but she had the maturity of a woman of about thirty-five.

Carol: I felt Robert was someone I could still be comfortable with when I was feeling my worst. I thought to myself, this is someone I could be sick with. There is a lot to be said for this.

*Laura Carroll*

*What is your life together like?*

Carol: In thirty-five years, we haven't run out of things to talk about.

Robert: We have a lot in common. We both read a lot. We like to go to the opera, symphony, museums, and ballet. We love to travel.

Carol: The things we have in common interest us in different ways. We enjoy trading ideas and sharing different perspectives.

We do lots of things separately too. We work out in different gyms. I love to cook, and can spend half the day at the farmers' market shopping for food.

Robert: I work a lot. I come into the office late and leave late. We have dinner together, and eat out about half of the time.

We each have our own study at home. I like to listen to jazz and classical music, and to play on the computer.

Carol: We have had the same housekeeper for over twenty years. When she is away, we divide up the domestics—except during tax season!

Robert: As you might guess, I handle our finances.

*Tell me about your circle of friends.*

Robert: When we first got married, we had a lot of single friends.

Carol: Some of them ended up having children. Some got married and did not have children. Other friends never did marry. Some of them finally came out of the closet, which, in our generation, was as difficult as not having children.

Over time, I lost touch with some of my friends because I moved, and our lifestyles became so different. The break had nothing to do with children. Geography was the major issue.

Robert: We have also developed friendships with older people whose children are grown. In a way, they are now like us, or we are like them.

*Tell me about your relationship with your cats.*

Robert: Many years ago, Carol took me to a bar and said we were getting a cat. After a few martinis, I agreed to get a cat. I had never been around a cat; I had dogs growing up, but the cat arrived, and I loved the cat.

Carol: I have had cats all of my life, but they are not part of the family. They are part of the household. We are not "mommy" and "daddy." They are our pets, not surrogate children on any level.

*What have been your biggest marital challenges?*

Carol: Early on, we survived my simultaneously going to college and working full-time. We survived parental death. Despite a lot of what has happened to us, we have had a remarkably even relationship.

Robert: I think it is because the marriage was based on the fact we got along from the start.

Carol: Probably the hardest thing for us was when I decided to go on a vacation by myself. I thought Robert was going to have a conniption!

Robert: Maybe I wasn't happy about it, but it was Carol's decision. She was going to do it anyway—there's not much I can do about it!

Carol: I need a little more space and time to be alone. It goes back to my childhood. In the beginning of our marriage, Robert did not understand this. I am not sure he understands it now, but he gives it to me.

*What are the ingredients to making it work over the long term?*

Robert: The most important thing is compatibility.

Carol: We started out liking a lot of the same things, and it has deepened over the course of our marriage.

Robert: We don't do things together because we are married; we do them because we each have a genuine interest in them.

*Laura Carroll*

Carol: And the things we have in common interest us in different ways. We trade ideas and share different perspectives.

It is also important to like different things. Marriage is not Siamese twin-ship. Couples are not joined at the hip!

Robert: Don't try to change the other person; let them be who they are.

Carol: Respect each other. Don't keep secrets. Don't carry a grudge, and recognize the reality that there are going to be days when you don't like him/her!

*In your opinion, how does society view the institution of marriage today?*

Carol: I think our generation perceives marriage differently. People got married and stayed married. The institution differs today because people do not get married for the rest of their lives.

Robert: Today, more people view marriage with the attitude of "Let's do it and see how it goes."

Carol: Even though the commitment isn't the same, I think there is an inherent human need for commitment and a warm body beside you. There is more of a biological urge for this than for procreation.

The social pressure to marry has changed too. When we got married, you couldn't live together. Society had it set up so you <u>had</u> to get married. You couldn't get an apartment lease if you weren't married.

Robert: Today, it is a lot easier to get married than it is to get unmarried. I think it should be the other way around. It should be difficult to get married and easier to get unmarried.

If I had the power to make it more difficult to get married, I'd experiment with some sort of required "trial" marriage period for couples to see if they are compatible. It would be like a marriage with an escape clause. After this, the couple could make another decision—to marry or to each take what they have and leave.

Carol: It is so important for younger people to recognize that marriage isn't the way we see it in the movies or in commercials. Marriage isn't always fun; it is a lot about being sick together, and taking one day at a time.

*Laura Carroll*

# CARLA AND NORM

The way I was treated as a child definitely
engendered my attitude toward having children.

-Norm

*C*arla and Norm have been married for twenty-three years.
Carla grew up in California, and Norm has lived in Oregon for
most of his life. They met at a party. Carla is a bookkeeper, and Norm
works as typesetter.

We met in their quaint home on a sunny Sunday morning. I sat in
their biggest, most comfortable chair that had enough room for one
of their cats to snuggle in next to me. They made great coffee, which
I savored as we talked.

~

*How did you decide that you did not want children?*

Carla: My mother had a big influence on why I decided not to have
children. She was a lousy parent. When I was a kid, I thought she was
crazy. I spent my whole life studying psychology, trying to find an
explanation for her. About ten years ago, I found a label in a psychology
book that described my mother—"narcissist personality disorder."

She was an unhappy person. Nothing was ever good enough, and
nothing made her happy. She was mean to us and didn't care about
me or my older brother and sister. She made it very clear we were "in

the way," and that if she had not had children, she could have been happy.

For a long time, I feared that if I had children, I would be mean like my mother. I had no idea how to mother any differently. I had a loving, caring father, but he died when I was too young to feel that I learned how to be a good parent. As a teenager, I made the decision that I would only have kids if I found a man who had good parents, wanted children, was good at parenting, and was willing to teach me.

Norm: The way I was treated as a child definitely engendered my attitude toward having children. Carla and I have lousy mothers in common. I didn't have a great father. He was an alcoholic; my parents fought and got violent. They divorced when I was nine.

My mother did totally inappropriate things—she got violent with me for no reason, and sexually abused me until I was about eleven. I knew it wasn't right but, at the time, had no way of objectively looking at the situation.

*Laura Carroll*

When I was about fifteen, I remember consciously deciding not to have children. I knew I didn't want to bring a child into my family. I could not stand the thought of my mother doing to any child what she had done to me. I felt powerless over her and that I had no prospect of getting away from her influence.

As I got older, my feelings about not having children got stronger. I felt that if I had a child, I wouldn't be strong enough to tell my mother that I would not allow her to have anything to do with him/her. I felt bad that I couldn't be honest with my mother, but speaking the truth broke a big rule in my family. I didn't feel capable of doing this for a long time.

Carla: We made the decision not to have children early in our relationship. We didn't feel confident that we would make good parents.

Norm: I had a vasectomy before we were married. We felt that if you're mistreated as a child, you'll end up mistreating your children. There was one sure way to prevent it, and that was not to have them to begin with. In a family situation, when things get stressful or feel out of control, people often revert to base behaviors.

Carla: People revert to what was done to them. Many people assume that "I won't be like my mother," or that "I'll do it differently than my parents"; but I didn't think like this—I feared I *would* be like her, and this fear drove my decision not to have children. I just knew at some point I would wake up and look in the mirror and realize that I was treating my child the way my mother treated me.

Norm: I never remember thinking I could do it better than my parents. It never occurred to me that I could be a good father. I always thought I didn't have the skills to teach a kid how to survive.

*Today, do you still feel you wouldn't be good parents?*

Carla: We're just now getting enough therapy under our belts, and have enough self-esteem that, right now, I think we could be good parents, but I'm in my late forties, and Norm is in his sixties—isn't it a bit late?

Norm: I still have my doubts that I would be a good parent. Kids terrify me. I don't feel I have the skills to relate to them. Maybe it's because when I was growing up, I had the responsibility of watching over my mother. I generally wasn't allowed to be a kid.

*Do you have any regrets about not having children?*

Carla: I would have loved to have had children. I regret that we weren't emotionally or psychologically ready enough at the right biological time. I don't think we made the wrong decision at the time. I would hate to be my age and have a couple of screwed-up kids.

Norm: I believe if we would have had kids, we probably wouldn't be together right now, and I would regret that. At the time, I don't think we were stable enough to take on parenthood.

Carla: I agree—if we would have thrown kids into the mix, I don't think we would have made it. We have worked very hard on ourselves and the relationship. It's much harder to do this when you have kids.

*Based on your experience, what perceptions does society have about married couples like you, who have consciously chosen not to parent?*

Carla: Generally speaking, not having children is nowhere near as big of a deal as it was twenty or fifty years ago. It's becoming more and more accepted.

Norm: I think couples like us are a reflection of society coming to terms with the reality that having children truly is a choice, but, in general, I don't think society has come to terms with children. We now have the choice to have them, yet so many people continue to have them for the wrong reasons. They do it because they feel their families expect them to have children, or just do it without thinking much about it.

*Laura Carroll*

*What are the biggest positives about not having children?*

Carla: Freedom! We can take a trip when we want to, or call each other at the end of the day and say, "Let's meet at a restaurant." I realized how much freedom we have when friends of ours had a child—all of a sudden they weren't available! For three years, we barely saw them because they were tied up at home with their child. When the child became a toddler, and we saw our friends, there were rules, like no more nude hot tubbing!

*Let's say a couple who is trying to decide whether they want children is asking your advice. What advice would you give to help them make their decision?*

Carla: I would tell them to do the "death bed test." I imagine myself ninety-seven years old, in a rest home, lying there dying, and thinking back over my life. I imagine myself thinking back to this moment—am I going to wish I did it this way, or wish I did it that way? In other words, I would ask them to ask themselves—"On my death-bed, will I wish I never had kids, or wish that I had?"

Norm: I would encourage them to look at themselves and how they were parented. I realize nobody has a perfectly happy child-hood, but I can't imagine anybody who had a healthy childhood not thinking someday that they would like to have children. I think a person raised in a healthy environment with healthy self-esteem will want to pass on something, and a child is the easiest way to do it.

When I see evidence that people are not caring for their children, I tend to make assumptions—like they really didn't want them in the first place, they took the decision to have them too lightly, or they did it before looking at themselves and past hurts. It's a scary place to go. So I would encourage them to take an honest look at the kind of parent they think they can and will be before deciding to have a child.

I'd advise them to ask themselves why they would want children. What need will it fulfill for themselves? Are they doing it for someone else? Most important, do they feel they have something to contribute to a child's happiness? Anybody can have a kid, but being a good parent is another ball-game.

*Laura Carroll*

*How did your love story begin?*

Carla: We met at a party. We left the party together, went dancing, and ended up at an all-night restaurant. We talked and drank coffee

until dawn. Not long after, we took a six-week back-packing trip. When we got back, we moved into together. We lived together for four years before we got married.

*Many couples get married when they're ready to start a family. This wasn't the case for you. Why did you get married?*

Carla: I was motivated by the fear that if anything happened to him, it would be like the movie "All That Jazz"—I'd rush to the hospital, and they wouldn't let me in to see him because "I'm not family." It's not like this anymore, but it was like that twenty-five years ago. It terrified me.

Norm: At the time I met Carla, I had been divorced and single for three years. I had been looking for a woman like her, but after lots of dating, I had nearly given up the search. I had begun to think that her kind of woman didn't exist. I was looking for someone who thought fifteen minutes was enough time to get ready to go almost anywhere— someone intelligent, who valued more than the latest fashions and latest trinkets. Then one night at a party, there she was. I fell in love. Four years later we were still together. I was waking up to the possibility of losing her if I didn't offer her something more permanent than a live-in relationship. She left to visit relatives in California for a few days, and when she got home, I asked her to marry me.

*What is your life together like?*

Carla: When we're not working, we enjoy working in the yard and hiking together. We like taking weekends away. I love to read and to arrange flowers. I like to try new things; right now, I am training to walk a marathon.

Norm: We live a fairly quiet life. We spend time with friends, and go out to dinner and movies, but we're at home a lot. I love to sit at my drawing table and draw what comes to me. I love to read too.

*How do you handle various aspects of the day-to-day things in marriage, for example, domestics and money management?*

Norm: Ever since we moved in together, we have had three bank

*Laura Carroll*

accounts. She has hers, I have mine, and we have the "household" account. We contribute a certain percentage of our income to our household account, and that's what we live on. The rest is ours to do with as we please.

Carla: My parents did not give me money as a kid. When I got old enough to earn a living, it was important to me to have my own money. I didn't want to give that up.

Other domestic sorts of things did not come naturally—we fought over them for years! Clutter continues to be an issue. I have to admit, I contribute to the clutter. I am not tidy; on my own I can just barely break even with clutter and tidiness. Throw Norm in, and the clutter is too much! I don't have enough compulsive tidiness to make up for his clutter-ness. It's a constant battle.

Norm: Carla is very good at dealing with problems like these when they come up. When a problem reaches a certain critical mass . . .

Carla: . . . I drag him kicking and screaming into a solution!

Norm: She wants to deal with it and make a plan to solve it. A lot of times it's not easy, because she forces me to look at things I really don't feel comfortable dealing with. We get better at it all the time.

*What have been your biggest marital challenges?*

Norm: My sexually abused past left me with a lot of sexual hang-ups. I have gone through a long process of working through them.

Carla: In 1984, we had a rough time. I was giving serious thought to leaving the marriage. Norm had just revealed more to me about his mother and childhood sexual background. He didn't trust me enough to tell me the truth about his sexual background for about twelve years.

During this struggle, one of the guys I worked with who'd been married almost thirty years reminded me that, "You can't expect a marriage not to have its ebbs and flows. When it's in an ebb, you have to have faith that it'll come back. Yes, it's horrible now, but it won't be horrible forever. You have to hang in there." His words saved me.

Norm: I learned the hard way that I had to drop my defenses and be honest with Carla, regardless of what the consequences might be, or what I *thought* they might be. When I did, Carla's responses amazed me. She responded with interest and with much less negativity than I expected.

*What ingredients have made your marriage work over the long term?*

Norm: It has taken a willingness to be honest about the things that are difficult to be honest about. I discovered that in order for Carla to have a relationship with me, she has to know who the "me" is, and if I withhold information about me, she doesn't have a chance. She can't have a relationship with someone who isn't revealing himself to her.

*In your opinion, how does society view the institution of marriage today?*

Norm: People continue to marry to announce their coming together, to build a home together, with children or not. The relationship is what it's all about. I have lots of relationships, but my relationship with Carla is deeper and more meaningful.

Carla: People have the urge to bond. We marry to joyously announce to the world we're bonded.

Marriage is not so much about family as it is about relationship. Marriage is not a prerequisite for having children. Marriage and parenting really are two separate things. I've seen couples who aren't married, have had a child, seem to enjoy sharing the child, even though they live independent lives, and aren't necessarily connected.

I don't think marriage is necessary to parent well. There are a lot of kids with single parents who get a much better start in life than I did. One good parent is a whole lot better than two lousy ones.

*Laura Carroll*

# JACKIE AND CRAIG

To me, the decision means thinking through all the
responsibilities you have to take on to raise the child and
determining whether you are willing to take them on, *as
well as* making your spouse the number one priority.

-Jackie

*J*ackie and Craig have been married for eleven years. They
both grew up in San Diego, and met through friends. They
work in the wireless communications industry; Jackie is in sales management, and Craig works in finance. We met in their living room on
a sunny Sunday morning.

~

*How did you decide that you did not want children?*

Jackie: Before we got married, we talked about whether we wanted
children. We decided it wasn't something we absolutely wanted but
thought maybe at some point we would.

Craig: Neither of us had strong feelings either way. We wanted to
wait and make the decision later. We both agreed that if we ever had
children, we would want to be able to give our child the same kind of
childhood that our parents gave us. Early in our marriage, this would
have been tough to do. We struggled to buy a home, and Jackie got
laid off. It was an easy decision at that point not to have kids. As we

established our careers and finances, we could have taken on the responsibility of children but chose not to.

As our marriage went on, we talked about it once in awhile and still didn't feel that we had a burning desire to have children. We were into our careers, and having a child would have been a huge sacrifice for both of us. We also didn't want to change our lifestyle.

I take my hat off to couples who have them. I don't know how they manage their careers, raise children, and stay together. We try to focus on each other, and it's still hard <u>without</u> kids. Maybe it scared me a little to think how children would affect our relationship.

*Families of Two*          ∴ 97 ∻

Jackie: The relationship can easily suffer because everything centers around the kids. I've seen couples who spend all of their time with their kids and too little with just themselves. I have heard friends and family members talk about how they choose not to do something or go somewhere because of their children. I could just see us arguing over who was going to take the child to, or pick the child up from, day care; take the child to the doctor; or stay home because the child was sick.

Craig: We'd have to decide whose meeting schedule for that day was less important. This would be difficult.

Jackie: Why would we want to put ourselves through this? We have a good thing now. Why would we want to try to screw it up?

Craig: I have seen how parenthood stresses people's relationships. We think kids would put a stress on our relationship, and it is not something we are willing to give up.

*Is there anything about you or your background that you think might have influenced you not to want children?*

Jackie: I was not one of those little girls who thought she wanted to be a mom. I was a tomboy and always knew I wanted to have a career. That's what I thought about when I was a girl. I thought about being married, but I never thought I was going to have children—never. It was just not in my makeup.

I was not brought up being told that having babies was what I was going to do when I grew up. My mom was not a typical housewife. She was always home, took me to my baseball and football games, but played the stock market all day!

Craig: We both had family role models who set the example that work was very important. My mom was home until my sister and I were old enough to stay by ourselves; then she went back to work part-time in the family business.

The family business made life comfortable for the family. They

*Laura Carroll*

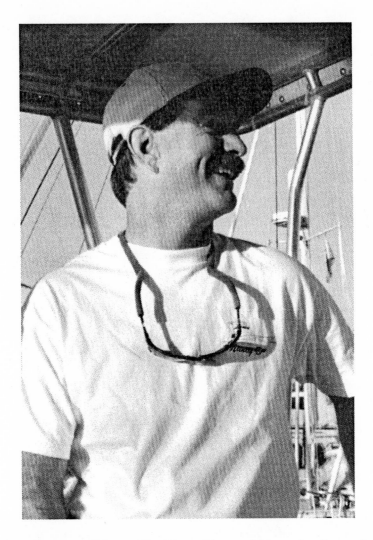

provided very well for us. I had lots of fun as a kid; our family traveled, camped, and took ski trips.

Jackie: My family had a nice lifestyle too. I had a great childhood. I think having it good as we grew up helped us see we had choices in life.

Craig: I think being raised to be independent had an influence. My parents always allowed me to make my own decisions.

Jackie: My parents also taught me to be independent and to take care of myself.

Craig: We grew up with minds of our own, so the decision to have children was up to us. We certainly weren't going to do it for our family, or just because most of our friends were having kids.

*Do you have any regrets about not having children?*

Jackie: We talk a lot about what is going to happen in the future.

Craig: We are planning for the future, but not waiting for the future. We know that, at anytime, something could happen to either one of us. We figure we have to live life while we can. We are trying to continue the lifestyle we had when we were growing up. A lot of people have to wait until the kids are out of college before they are able to travel or do what they want to do. Fortunately, having good jobs enables us to afford to do the things we like to do, when we like to do them.

*Let's say a couple who is trying to decide whether they want children is asking your advice. What advice would you give to help them make their decision?*

Jackie: To me, the decision means thinking through all the responsibilities you have to take on to raise the child and determining whether you are willing to take them on, *as well as* making your spouse the number one priority.

Craig: I would tell them to think through the costs and responsibilities of raising a child beforehand. A lot of people don't sit down and figure out how much money it is going to take, or how it will affect their lifestyle. How much will it cost to clothe and feed the child? Day care? Education as she/he grows up? Will one spouse quit working? When these things aren't planned for, the couple can encounter real financial strain, which can lead to relationship problems.

*Laura Carroll*

*What perceptions do you think other people have of you, as a couple that has chosen not to have children?*

Craig: We don't go around broadcasting that we don't want kids. If someone we don't know well asks us, we say we still haven't made the decision, even though in our minds we know we aren't going to have them. It is just easier to side-step the issue than to have to explain why to people.

Jackie: I think most people are a little surprised we have chosen not to have kids. It still seems to be more abnormal than normal.

Craig: But I have never gotten the feeling others think we are weird. When people ask how we afford the boat, I say, "It's our kid!" Often, they have never thought of it this way.

Jackie: I think some parents are envious because they see us do things, buy things, or travel. We can be spontaneous. They can't be.

I have asked a number of parents if they would do it all over again and they said, "Absolutely not." They said they wouldn't trade their kids for anything—they love them, and they're wonderful, but if they had to do it over again, they wouldn't do it. My father has even said this to me!

Craig: I bet if you asked men without their families around if they would do it over again, a high percentage of them would say they wouldn't. I don't think a lot of men have a burning desire to have kids. Some do, but more don't, in my opinion. I don't think our social programming to have children is as strong as it is for women.

*How do you see yourselves as different from people who have children?*

Jackie: People who have children have chosen to increase their responsibilities and lose some of their independence.

Craig: Their choices are certainly more limited than if they had chosen not to have children.

Jackie: I see lots of parents who make themselves and their spouses a low priority most of the time, instead of balancing self, spouse, and children. Because everything centers around the children, they often forget what they really want to do in their own lives.

*What do you see as your role in molding the next generation of children?*

Jackie: We can help educate children that they need to make their own decisions. They need to learn to be independent. I encourage young people a lot to do their own thing, and not what others expect them to do. I think this helps them learn who they are and what they want out of life.

Craig: Many young people are pressured by their families about their education, career, marriage, and children. We can impress upon them that they shouldn't worry about what others think, especially their family and friends. They need to live their own lives.

Jackie: We can also encourage kids to go to college. College can really help increase self-esteem, which many young people need. I did not go to college out of high school, and wished I would have. It was important to me to get my degree, and I finally finished it a few years ago.

Craig: It took me eight years to finish my degree. I worked at menial jobs while going to school and got tired of them. This gave me the momentum to get out of college and pursue my career.

*Tell me how your love story began.*

Craig: One of my friends was dating Jackie's hairstylist, and they thought we would hit it off.

Jackie: We went water skiing on our first date. I'll never forget standing in the sand with my water ski, waiting for this guy I had met only once to come around the corner in a boat.

We were pretty inseparable from that point forward. I knew after two weeks I was going to marry him. We dated for a year before moving in together. Because neither of us believed in living together for a long time, we had a deal that we'd give it six months. We figured we'd

*Laura Carroll*

know by then whether or not we wanted to get married. After living together for three months, we decided to get married.

*What is your life together like?*

Jackie: I like to ride the Stair-master in the morning. He goes to the gym. During the week, we work all day.

I plan our meals during the week. They are simple because I hate to cook. During the week, we make dinner at home.

Craig: Over dinner, we often listen to Jackie's day, because Jackie's days are always much more exciting than mine!

Jackie: Whoever doesn't make dinner cleans it up. Then we'll watch a bit of television. I watch it to unwind, and stop thinking about work. Sometimes, I work in the evening.

Craig: She isn't the type to relax.

Jackie: I don't relax. It is just not me. He is the even-keeled one. I am the Type A; he is more Type B.

Craig: Our money is together; I pay the bills and manage our finances.

Jackie: I ask for reports on the finances so that I know what is going on. He takes the lead on the yard. I do the laundry.

Craig: We are not messy people. When it got to the point when we were spending our weekends cleaning, we decided we didn't want to do that. So we got a housecleaner.

Jackie: As far as hobbies go, if it were up to me, being a workaholic Type A, my hobby would be to work seven days a week.

Craig: I constantly have to tell her to stop on the weekends.

Jackie: For fun we deep sea fish, golf, and snow ski. We generally take about two vacations a year. We like to go to Mexico.

Craig: Ultimately, we'd like to have a large yacht fisher and travel on it. If we play our cards right, we should be able to retire in our fifties, but Jackie says she doesn't want to retire. So I have this picture that when we get to our mid-fifties, I will retire, while she will continue to work and consult from somewhere in Mexico.

*What is your circle of friends like?*

Craig: These days, we hardly see friends who have started families since we have been married.

Jackie: We see more of our friends who don't have children. We are good friends with one couple who has no children and has been married twenty-two years. We ski and go to Mexico together.

Craig: We also spend a lot of time with members of our families. Both Jackie and I have small families, so we are very close to them. We all live in the same city.

*Tell me about your relationship with your cat.*

Jackie: She is part of the family, and everybody loves her.

Craig: She makes us laugh.

Jackie: She makes me cry. She has such a personality. She is not one of those cats that hide under the bed. She is very friendly and likes to talk to us all of the time. She is getting old, and when she has to move on, that is going to be very hard.

*What have been your biggest marital challenges?*

Craig: We have had little bumps like any couple but haven't had any tough times.

Jackie: I think it is because we are each other's best friends.

Craig: We have learned to make sure we spend enough time together.

Jackie: My parents were married for forty-two years before my mom died, and her advice to me on the day we got married was to be sure we did things together.

Craig: We have gone through times when we have been very busy with our careers and tended to neglect each other. We would get caught up in work and not tell each other how much we love each other. Sometimes, we would wait too long before we got away from it all. Getting away helps us refocus on each other. I have a rule when we travel: The laptop does not go with her!

Jackie: I have learned to accept how much fishing is part of Craig's life. He grew up with it. I know we will always have a boat.

Craig: I don't even have to be out fishing on it. I can spend a whole weekend just working on it. I'd do it every weekend if she'd let me!

*In your opinion, how does society view the institution of marriage today?*

Craig: Many people still believe the misconception that marriage and babies go hand in hand.

Jackie: It is a commitment that says we are responsible for the marriage and for making sure it continues.

Craig: Religion still plays a huge role in marriage today. Marrying someone of the same religion remains very important to lots of people.

Jackie: We aren't religious. We meditate on the boat with a margarita! I didn't grow up with any kind of religion.

Craig: I had to go to church when I was young, but it didn't play much of a role in my life. We have trouble with religions that dictate one's values. We firmly believe everyone should have the right to make the choices they want to make. Religions too often set up these choices for people.

Jackie: Social factors are influencing choices about marriage and children too. Because a lot of children are growing up in one-parent families, in the future maybe we won't see marriage as often as we once did. Coming from a one-parent background may set a different example as the norm.

Craig: The population coming out of college now doesn't think they have to get married right away—it is not in their mindset. There isn't a huge rush anymore. These days, I less often see kids who don't go to college and marry early. More children are being raised in homes where both parents work, and this can influence what they will do when they become adults.

Jackie: They may see work as more important than having a family, at least when they are younger. I know that, for many women today, there is more to life than just motherhood. I think this is very important. I see more young women going to college straight from high school these days, instead of getting married right away and starting a family.

If women are going to have children and decide to be stay-at-home moms, it is crucial that they have a skill or education, in case they end up on their own, raising their children by themselves. I have seen too many women who married early in life, had children, did not establish a career outside the home, got divorced, and then struggled hard to make ends meet to continue the lifestyle they once had.

Craig: Ten to twenty years from now, I bet the percentage of those who choose not to have children will be much higher. Now, most people in our society have one or two children. The average is coming down. As more people choose not to have children, these averages will come down even further.

# INGRID AND BOB

I can't say that if I had my life to do over again,
I would have had kids. It's this life I'd want to live over
again—a life that has constantly challenged me to bring
myself out in the open.

-Bob

*I*ngrid and Bob have been married for thirty-three years. They grew up in St. Louis, Missouri, and met in high school through mutual friends. Ingrid is the resident director of a community called Blue Sky Ranch. She is also an astrologer and leads workshops on spirituality topics. Bob works as an attorney. We met on a sunny, spring morning at their home on Blue Sky Ranch, which sits perched on a hillside, facing miles of mountains.

~

*How did you decide that you did not want children?*

Ingrid: I came to my own decision. It wasn't something I pondered and pondered. I never felt compelled to have a child. I have three siblings, and the last one came thirteen years after the one before. My father was a musician and was never home at night because he was working. Reflecting on my mother's life, I think she felt she raised the children by herself. It was obvious that she was not a fulfilled person. She loved us, but a whole aspect of her woman-ness wasn't happening.

Bob is a lot like my father. He is very career oriented, and not home very much. I didn't want to live my life the way my mother lived hers.

Bob: I did not have a burning desire. It would have been fine if we had had them, and just as fine not to have had them, but I had my feelings about kids. When I was growing up, I saw the impact that kids had on my mother and father. We had five kids in our family, and my father worked very hard to provide for us. His life was pretty thankless; I don't think he was a happy man.

My father never went to college, but my mother did. She was a linguist, and as soon as she started to have kids, all of that went out the window. One hundred percent of her life went into her family. She loved being a mom, but she gave up everything else. I watched her waste her education, but she gave us great values and made education a priority in our household.

It seemed to me that the woman bore the brunt of raising the kids. I didn't want Ingrid to live the type of life my mom had lived. I also felt there were already so many people in the world. The violence in the world influenced me too. People talked a lot about nuclear war when I was growing up. I felt it was not a very good environment to bring children into.

Ingrid: I never felt it wasn't a good time to bring children into the world. I believe in reincarnation, and that a soul comes to the world it wants to come into. My astrological chart shows that this lifetime is about wrapping up previous relationships. Many of the people who live in this community were my children and family members in other lifetimes. I know this sounds out there—I was rather skeptical myself, but as I've explored it, I have uncovered lots of memories from past lives.

*It's widely held that women have children because they are fulfilling a natural biological urge. What do you think about this?*

Ingrid: I agree. It is a hormonally supported species survival instinct. Personally, I like the way children were raised in tribal cultures. The young people who had the physical stamina gave birth to the children, who were then communally raised and educated by the elders, the theory being that the mature members of the tribe could pass down the wisdom gained through their experiences. To me, this is a great way to raise children. Too bad we're far from this now.

As we get older, our base of wisdom broadens, and we're able to see more of the realistic picture of what it means to have a child. There are probably many parents who, had they seen this picture and

*Laura Carroll*

thought it through, would have elected not to have children; but having children is culturally expected, and hormonally supported, so there's a pretty strong current there.

*Let's say a couple who is trying to decide whether they want children is asking your advice. What advice would you give to help them make their decision?*

Bob: I think, like every answer in life, it lies within us. To get to it, we have to know ourselves. It's a long journey, and it can take a lifetime. We have to develop the talent to listen to ourselves. Most of the difficulty that we run into in life stems from the fact that we don't listen to ourselves. The inner-self is always giving us information. It's an art form for the outer-self to appreciate what the inner-self is telling us, and to act on it.

Ingrid: To help them know themselves, they need to take time to make friends with themselves, just like they would with anyone else. Too often, people go too fast in life and make important decisions in traffic—"in between" life, so to speak.

If they find they need to have kids to feel they have lived a useful life, then they ought to have kids. If they think that it's not what they need in this lifetime, perhaps that's a good reason not to have kids.

*What perceptions do you think others have of you, as a couple who has chosen not to have children?*

Bob: We're the only ones in my family who don't have children. For a while, they thought it was unusual. I was born in 1942, and in my generation, it was very uncommon not to follow the same pattern as your parents. You got married young, had kids, raised kids, worked hard all of your life, retired, and watched your kids raise their kids. Now, it's less unusual not to want children.

Ingrid: I would never look at a couple and draw an opinion about their private life, so I've never thought someone might be looking at me and doing this! I have never felt judged in any way, but no one ever asked us to baby-sit. Maybe they thought we wouldn't have known how to deal with it.

*Do you have any regrets about not having children?*

Bob: When I'm around my brother's and sister's kids, I see in vivid detail what it could have been like. They have wonderful kids, and they are so proud of them, and there's so much heartache—which might be a plus for not having kids!

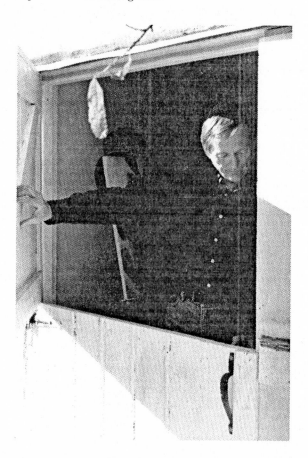

*Laura Carroll*

I can't say that if I had my life to do over again, I would have had kids. It's this life I'd want to live over again—a life that has constantly challenged me to bring myself out in the open.

Ingrid: No regrets. If I had had children, I don't think I would have had enough energy left to do what I'm doing with people here at Blue Sky Ranch. Rather than a nuclear family, I have found an extended family arrangement instead.

*What do you see as your role in molding the next generation?*

Ingrid: To assist and help. I feel values and ethics are a real problem with this generation of children. Everyone could get on the bandwagon and help—through volunteering in organizations like Big Brother, or Planned Parenthood, or teaching children through programs offered by local parks, museums, and educational facilities.

Bob: Everyone, with or without children, has an obligation to mentor young people. I was well mentored—I think it's how kids learn values. Today's kids have big distractions, like the entertainment industry. Often, parents work a lot and have less time and energy for it.

*How did your love story begin?*

Bob: Ingrid was dating my best friend, and I was dating a woman he knew. We double dated. Ultimately, we changed partners—he married the woman I dated, and I married Ingrid!

*What is your life together like?*

Ingrid: A large part of it revolves around managing Blue Sky Ranch.

Bob: We're constantly working together and making decisions pertaining to the Ranch. We also get involved in community issues, like battling to save a canyon from development. We also manage a rental home and have a small place in the desert. These things, coupled with my legal work—it's a lot to handle.

Ingrid: We also have regular date nights; we go to dinner, to the movies, or visit with friends.

*How did you come to create Blue Sky Ranch?*

Ingrid: We founded it thirteen years ago. Before then, I was a glass artist. A woman who worked for me told me about a study group she was with that was like a community. I started participating, and then Bob started going. We made friends with this community of people and got used to "community" as a lifestyle. Then we lived there for a year.

I continued to work with the concept of self-actualization and studied different belief systems. I have always been a spiritual person. When I was in high school, when all of the girls were looking at the boys, I was in church giving myself to God!

Blue Sky Ranch was created as a spiritual community, with no single definition of the word "spiritual." The Community goal is to help each person develop him or herself in a way that is consistent with his/her "spiritual truth."

*What does life at Blue Sky Ranch entail?*

Ingrid: There are many facets to it. Right now, eleven people live here, and about ten come up on the weekends and for workshops. The Community is self-supporting. The people who live here pay rent. We have approximately 2000 fruit trees, and we sell the fruit. We have a community garden, and everyone chips in each month for food and utility expenses. We share a common kitchen. There is a menu planner and a food shopper. There is a different cook each night. We rotate common area maintenance duties. Each person takes care of his or her living space.

We address the spiritual aspect of life through forms of meditation and ritual. Some people sit on a rock; others sit in front of an

*Laura Carroll*

altar—they do whatever works for them. The goal is to get in touch with your own God, however you define It, and to bring yourself into an intentional relationship with that God. We have a saying that describes the process, "Make your life your ritual."

In the evenings and on weekends, there are lectures, workshops, and projects. People work together, with the support of others who are also dedicated to improving themselves and to living in harmony with nature and their spiritual intent.

*Tell me about your circle of friends.*

Ingrid: We have a social life outside the Community that looks "normal." Our friends include mostly astrology and law business colleagues.

Bob: Our friends don't ever ask us why we didn't have kids. They also don't ask us, "How is your community going?" Many of them don't understand the community lifestyle.

Ingrid: They just say, "What have you been doing?" and hope we don't say much! We originally went into a community setting in the seventies, and then it was weird. Now, I have a handful of friends who know about our community life and think it's cool. That handful is getting larger. People are changing. They're opening up to it.

*Why do you think you came together in this life?*

Bob: It's probably because of some unfinished business from a prior lifetime. There are things I can help Ingrid with, and things she can help me with.

Ingrid has made me a much better person than I would have otherwise been. She helped open a lot of doors for me. Had I not met her, I would have married my college girlfriend, and be living in the St. Louis suburbs with five kids. I would have followed in my father's footsteps and probably have been as miserable as he was.

Ingrid: We have exposed one another to different lives. Bob takes me to his world. I take him into my world. We've meshed them together.

Bob: If you wanted to focus on our differences, you'd see many of them, and reason enough for us to say good-bye to one another. We choose not to do this. We know there is a common purpose for us to be together, and it's very fulfilling for both of us.

*What have been the biggest lessons you have learned in being together?*

Bob: I have learned how to listen to myself and others. At one point in my life, I was pretty closed-minded. I was raised Catholic and had tunnel vision of how things should be. With Ingrid, that tunnel vision began to expand. I began to relate to people differently. I started to better understand what they're dealing with, the things that affect them, and how they're struggling with life, as we all do. I just didn't have this kind of connection with people before. I began to understand that there's a spiritual quality about all of us and that others are working on themselves like I am. Knowing this has given me a sense of why I'm here and what I'm supposed to do in this lifetime. I think I am here to use the talents God has given me to help others. Life is about passing information on and helping each other.

I can almost exclusively relate what I have learned to my relationship with Ingrid. If this part of me was there before, I repressed it, and Ingrid brought it out. I owe her the most important part of my life.

Ingrid: Bob taught me to be independent. As you see me sitting here now, you would think I'm a headstrong, independent person, but when I got married, I wasn't. It was buried somewhere inside me.

He has always sent the message, "Don't look to me to find out how you should think; you can do it yourself." He has always pushed me in this way, and sometimes I hated it!

My independence has also been a big source of problems for us—

Bob: I don't want you to have the impression that I was this open-minded person when Ingrid said she wanted to go off to a spiritual school and not see me two days a week. I had a big reaction to that and to the whole sense of community. It was not an easy transition for me, but I've always encouraged her to be her own person.

*Laura Carroll*

Families of Two     ～ 117 ～

It came directly from watching my mother give up so much of her identity. I encouraged Ingrid to go do what she wanted to do, and then she did! And when she did, at first I had a cow!

Ingrid: I could say the same thing. As he discovered and developed himself, I didn't always like what he decided to do either, but it's that corny old thing of "holding someone with an open hand." It's scary, but it's the only way to have a relationship.

We're thankful to one another for what we have learned. We have both loved and hated the process, but neither one of us would be who we are today if we hadn't had that push from the other one.

*What are the ingredients to making marriage work over the long term?*

Ingrid: Communication.

Bob: We're still working on this one. I think it's common with many men—I get quiet and don't communicate a lot.

Ingrid: And I over-communicate. I say, "C'mon, give me the feeling!" In marriage, people have to tell the other person their feelings, perspectives, and what they need.

Bob: But we often can't provide what the other person needs. Neither of us have supplied anywhere near 100% of what the other person needed throughout our relationship.

Ingrid: What an unrealistic expectation!

Bob: Lots of people can't accept this, and the relationship ends. It's important in a relationship to say, "I am not going to get all that I need from the other person. What am I going to do about it?"

*In your opinion, how does society view the institution of marriage today?*

Bob: Today, marriage has many faces, like same-sex marriage, and living together. In the coming generations, I believe more people may not honor the legal system of marriage because of the perceived punishment dealt out to them if it turns out that, in the eyes of the legal system, they made a wrong choice. The legal system is set up with the message that if you make a bad choice, there are consequences.

Ingrid: These days, in addition to marriage, more people are saying things like, "I'm in a committed relationship." Marriage is not the commitment it used to be. When we got married, people didn't divorce. I got married, intending to be with this man my whole life; I never thought about being divorced. That's the way I was raised.

Now, more people don't feel this way at all. The way they see it, they're together for growth, not for life. I am not sure how I feel about this. I doubt that I would have stayed around for as much "growth" as I have experienced in my marriage if I had not made a serious commitment at the beginning. Then again, I have many friends who are on their second or third marriages, and they feel that each one is better than the last. I guess, like everything else in life, it is up to the individual.

# SHOSHANA AND DAVID

When we considered what it would take to have kids,
it just didn't seem worth it.

-David

$\mathcal{S}$ hoshana and David have been married eighteen years.
They met in Israel, when they were both teaching there.
Shoshana grew up in Connecticut, and David is from New York.

Shoshana is a painter, and works in acrylic on clear plastic. She is also the assistant director, operations analysis, for a city transit authority. David is a poet and translator of Hebrew poetry. He has a master's in international affairs and a master's in creative writing. He has also completed doctoral courses in comparative literature. His poems and translations have appeared in magazines, including The *Massachusetts Review, Passages North, The Literary Review, Archipelago,* and *Chelsea.* He has completed two books of poems entitled, *Glued to the Sky,* and *JFK: Lines of Fire,* and has translated a book of poems by an Israeli poet. David also promotes Shoshana's work to galleries and through Internet art auctions. We met in their loft-style apartment on a Saturday afternoon.

~

*How did you decide that you did not want children?*

David: It wasn't something we systematically thought out. Our decision evolved for a number of reasons.

Shoshana: When we left Israel, I was questioning it. I was approaching thirty, and felt that if I were going to have children, I wanted to do it when I was reasonably young; but. I didn't feel a great need to have kids and couldn't find an overriding reason to have them. Growing up, I never baby-sat kids. I have never changed a diaper in my life. I don't relate well to babies. I realized I didn't want a child enough to endure all the discomforts. I dislike the idea of pregnancy; I have no desire to experience morning sickness, weight gain, back pains, and swollen legs, with relief coming only after the pain of childbirth. Then there are midnight feedings, lost sleep, dirty diapers, and the potential of post partum depression.

Plus, my vanity discourages me from doing anything that would change my figure. Many women have such difficulty returning to their figures after childbirth.

David: Two things made an impression on me before we left Israel. We became friends with a couple who was ten years older than we are. They chose not to have children and were our first role models of this choice. They once told us that they felt their friends became boring once they had kids.

In a candid moment, another couple with three kids said they had the best years of their marriage before their first child was born. A light went on in my head—if that's the case, why bother?!

Shoshana: The constant demands of caring for my brother's autistic child confirmed any second thoughts I might have had after we decided we weren't going to have children. I saw how you can't assume your child will be healthy, and that you just don't know what kind of demands your child will make of you.

The fact that I earn most of the income also influenced our decision. Having children would have put an extra strain on me.

David: When we considered what it would take to have kids, it just didn't seem worth it.

*It's widely held that women have children because they are fulfilling a natural biological urge. What do you think about this?*

David: I think Shoshana and I can separate the biological urge to have sex and the biological urge to reproduce.

Shoshana: I have not had it. Is it a natural urge, or just engrained ways from the past? Historically, the need to procreate was economic. Now, it's almost the opposite—economics often acts as a negative incentive these days.

*Is there anything about your background that you think might have influenced you not to want children?*

David: It may have had to do with the "head of household" example I had growing up. I remember my father worked constantly. He took on extra teaching jobs to support us and was either at work, or at home grading papers. As a kid, I realized I didn't want any part of this. Even if my father was there physically, he wasn't always there mentally, or emotionally.

I got my share of caring for children growing up. I am the oldest of five and cared a lot for my brothers and sister. Sibling rivalry may have also influenced me. It played a big part in the psychology of my childhood. My parents had one kid after another, and each one took more attention away from me.

Shoshana: I am the third generation of women on my father's side of the family who didn't have children. My father's sister is rather unconventional. She has lived in many places, has had different types of jobs, and even changed her name. She set the stage for me in a lot of ways. I changed my name as well from Susan to my Hebrew name, Shoshana.

*What do you think of the notion of having kids so you will have someone to take care of you when you're old?*

David: It's a vestigial thing from an earlier economic system.

Shoshana: There are no guarantees in life—and is it fair to say to a kid, "I am bringing you into this world so you can one day take care of me?"

*Let's say a couple who is trying to decide whether they want children is asking your advice. What advice would you give to help them make their decision?*

Shoshana: They need to be able to clearly articulate why they want to have children. I think too many people don't think about why they want to have children before they have them.

David: Before they make their decision, I would advise them to spend a week with a family of kids to see what it's really like.

*What impressions do you think others have of you, as a couple that has chosen not to have children?*

Shoshana: I don't think others quite figure us out. They may think we can't have children and can't afford to do in vitro or adoption.

David: They are curious—it's the question they'd love to ask but know they shouldn't.

Shoshana: Someone once said to me, "That's so selfish of you!" I think it's more that people feel threatened when they see a happy couple without children. It questions the basis of this strong desire in them. The desire could very well come from how we are conditioned to have them from an early age. As kids, how many times do we hear, "Wait until you have your own children!" We are sent the message that having children is just part of life, so when you don't have them, you are questioning a basic tenet of society.

David: From a larger perspective, the tax laws seem to send the message that we haven't gotten with the program, that we're not following the game plan.

Shoshana: Economic growth drives the system, which means population growth. The system seems to send the message, "We need more people to fill more jobs; never mind the problems a growing population creates."

*Laura Carroll*

*What have been the best things about not having children?*

David: I have been able to live a literary life, and we don't have the expense that children require.

Shoshana: If we had had kids, I don't think I would have been able to paint. Work, paint, kids—it would be too much.

*What has been toughest about not having kids?*

Shoshana: Trying to explain why we don't have kids. One of my favorite things to say is, "We kept trying, but somehow David just didn't seem to be able to get pregnant!"

*Were you ever pressured to have children?*

Shoshana: Luckily, our families have been very good about it. Your brother—May he rest in peace—didn't accept our decision more than anyone.

David: My brother couldn't quite understand our decision not to have children. He was gay, and there was a side to him that would have loved to have had kids. He also wanted to conform; he wanted to be an "all-American regular guy" who happened to be gay. His desire to conform made it harder for him to understand why we would choose not to.

*Do you see yourselves as different than the mainstream?*

David: A mainstream couple is likely to have a couple of kids with both spouses working. This is not us.

Also, a lot of people make life about making as much money as they can, and then trying to live as high of a lifestyle as that money will support.

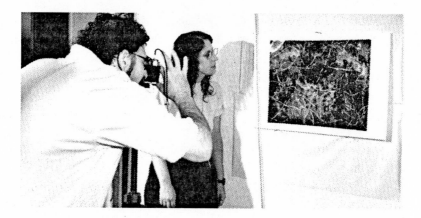

Shoshana: It's not that we would object to having more money, but we aren't as materialistic as the norm.

David: Being a poet is not mainstream. I don't know if I chose it, or it chose me. I love the writing of it, the arrangement of words, and finding the right music in the language to suit what I'm trying to say. This relates to translation as well, because it's about re-creating a poem in a new language.

Shoshana: In our religious community we are a real aberration. Very few people in our synagogue don't have children. If we went to an Orthodox synagogue, it would pose a real conflict; we would be looked upon with disdain.

We go to an untraditional synagogue. It is affiliated with the Jewish Conservative movement, which falls somewhere in the middle of the Reform movement and Orthodox tradition. In the early twentieth century, the Conservative movement was formed to "conserve" the tradition, yet not be Orthodox.

David: Our synagogue has a fairly traditional liturgy, but completely egalitarian gender roles.

*What do you see as your role in molding the next generation of children?*

David: At our synagogue, the children are everybody's children.

When a kid needs help, or is doing something wrong, the closest adult attends to it. The kids feel like family to us.

Shoshana: I allow children to see a life without children. I model how to contribute to the lives of children without having my own. I have a special relationship with two sweet boys at synagogue who have limited adult role models. I think I fill a need for them. Giving them love and support fills a need in me too.

*How did your love story begin?*

Shoshana: We met while we were living in Israel, in a program that roughly compares to the Peace Corps.

David: We were teaching in different small towns. I was teaching English in a junior high school, and Shoshana was teaching Hebrew literacy to women who could not read or write.

We met on a tour of a portion of the Sinai that was still under Israeli control at the time. I spotted Shoshana on the bus, and we went for a walk that evening.

Shoshana: By the end of the trip, we were definitely "an item" people were talking about!

David: After the trip, we visited each other on weekends. A few months later, we moved in together in the town she was living in. Within about three months, we got engaged. A few months later, we went back to the United States for the wedding, and then returned to Israel to go to graduate school.

Shoshana: We lived in Israel for the first three years of our marriage, and then moved back to the United States.

*What is your life together like?*

Shoshana: I go to work early during the week and usually leave about four o'clock. We have an early dinner, and sometimes we go for a walk. We exercise together regularly.

We do the marketing on Wednesday evenings, and on Thursday nights we cook up enough food for most of the week. It's easier to have most of the food already made during the week. I hate cooking on an empty stomach! Fridays we always have a nice evening meal together, sometimes with friends.

David: I write and transcribe poems at home. I am also the president of our building's co-op board, and supervise projects related to the building. We socialize on Friday evenings and Saturdays.

Shoshana: I paint on Sundays. I am very much a colorist. I work on the reverse side of the clear plastic and love the intensity of the resulting color on the front.

*How do you handle various aspects of the day-to-day things in marriage, for example, domestics and money management?*

David: We cook together and split doing the dishes. We generally share the cleaning.

Shoshana: I usually do the laundry. I keep the checkbook. David handles our investments and does the taxes.

David: We didn't put our money together until we were married eleven years and moved here. It just made more sense when we bought our home.

*Tell me about your circle of friends.*

David: A few of our friends have kids. Maybe I am reading into it, but when our friends have kids, I get a sense of disapproval, like we are shirking responsibility; or maybe it's just that we don't have as much in common anymore because children become such a big part of their lives.

Shoshana: Other friends have kids that are grown, so the kids don't dominate their lives anymore.

David: We often go to dinner with friends on Friday nights, or to lunch after synagogue on Saturday.

*Laura Carroll*

*What have been your biggest marital challenges?*

David: Early in our marriage before we left Israel, our marriage felt very stressed.

Shoshana: We started couple's therapy when we got back to the United States. We weren't communicating well—we each thought the other one wasn't happy, and wanted to leave Israel.

David: A few years later, we got into therapy again; we weren't communicating well at that time either. I got a job as a case-worker for a foster care agency and liked it, but Shoshana couldn't see me working in this kind of job.

Shoshana: I was afraid of burnout.

David: I resented the fact I quit that job because she wanted me to.

Shoshana: I felt David blamed me for his unhappiness. He was also realizing that he is a poet and that he didn't want to do a job he didn't like.

David: I started thinking about what I really want to do and applied to graduate school in creative writing.

Shoshana: It was a transition in which our marriage had to rework itself.

*What has been important to making it through difficult times?*

Shoshana: We got better at communicating our feelings. We each have worked on being in more in touch with how we're feeling, and communicating those feelings to each other.

David: We still go through rough patches, but having made it through previous challenges gives us faith and perspective.

*What are the ingredients that have made it work over the long term?*

David: We work to keep open channels of communication.

Shoshana: We have learned that keeping a relationship going sometimes means compromising. Our religion interests both of us very much. Having different levels of religiosity can be a problem with couples. Although we have slightly different perspectives on some issues, we have the same level of religiosity. For example, we are on the same wavelength regarding our level of observance on Passover.

*Tell me how you view the institution of marriage. What does being married mean to you?*

David: It's about companionship. It's wanting to be with the other person all the time. In a more formal religious context, entering into the institution of marriage sanctified our relationship.

Shoshana: We were married in the Reform synagogue in which I grew up, by the Rabbi I considered "my Rabbi" in high school and college. Although in the Reform synagogue, we chose to have a fairly traditional ceremony, and we had a standardized Ketubah, or wedding contract, from the Orthodox movement.

David: In the Orthodox tradition, a wedding contract, in a sense, is to protect the woman. There are certain obligations a man has towards the woman. In traditional Jewish practice, there is no such thing as alimony. The woman gets a lump sum at divorce. When the couple signs the wedding contract, they negotiate what that number is going to be. They sign the contract before the ceremony.

Every wedding contract states that a husband has to provide his wife with certain things, including sexual gratification. The Talmud even specifies how often he has to "service" her.

*Do you follow this Orthodox way in your marriage?*

Shoshana: I am definitely not complaining; that's all I'll say!

*Laura Carroll*

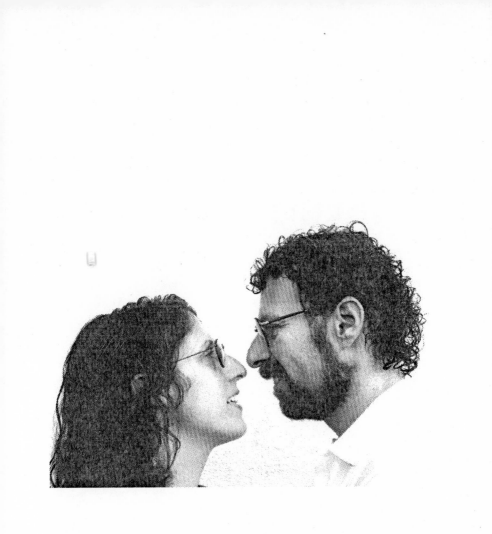

*Families of Two* .·. *131* .~

# CAROLE AND RICH

I think I would have been a great mom, but I wouldn't
have become who I have become.
-Carole

*C*arole and Rich have been married for eighteen years. Carole
is from Philadelphia, Pennsylvania, and Rich grew up in
Bethlehem, Pennsylvania. They met at a personal development seminar.
Rich worked in data processing before he became a postal carrier in
1991. Carole is a sign language interpreter, and has done singing
free-lance voice-over work for radio and television for over twenty
years. Carole and Rich have also been involved in local theater.

They were wonderful hosts. After taking me to a charming local
Italian restaurant for dinner, we went to their home with their four
lively cats. We talked in their living room.

~

*How did you decide you did not want to have children?*

Carole: We talked about it early in our relationship, and each
heard what we wanted the other one to say. I said that I didn't want
them right now, and that I might not ever, but I might. He heard me
say, "I don't want children." I heard him say he didn't want kids, but
that he might in the future. That wasn't really the case.

Two years after we were married, the topic came up again. We struggled with the decision for a few years. I wanted us to have children, and Rich did not.

A number of people said to me, "Just do it. Just don't put the diaphragm in; just get pregnant." I couldn't do this. I needed it to be a conscious choice for both of us. I needed him to say, "I want this with you." It had to be something we both wanted to do.

When my godson and niece were born, I thought, "There are babies in my life!"—and there are *just enough* babies in my life. I began to see I didn't need to have children all of the time, every day.

Later the same year that my godson and niece were born, I had an epiphany. One Saturday morning, I was taking my time waking up and did not have any place I had to be. It was as if God whispered in my ear, "Try looking at it this way. Look at what you can do. Look at what you've been able to do."

All of a sudden, my burning desire to have a child was gone. Before then, it hurt when I saw people with babies. I would think to myself, "I want one. Being a mother is part of who I am supposed to be."

*Families of Two*

∴ 133 ∾

50-CARR

After that morning, I recognized I could have been a mom but didn't have to be. It was a choice I could make. I also realized I could choose to continue to mourn the fact that I did not, and would not, have children, or I could learn to celebrate who I am without children, and all of the great things that go along with this. That day stimulated a big shift in my identity.

I think I would have been a great mom, but I wouldn't have become who I have become. There is so much I wouldn't have been able to do. I wouldn't have gone back to college the way I did. I couldn't be the wife that Rich needs. I would have been used up on somebody else. I don't think that would have been fair to him.

Rich: I always knew I did not want children. I gave a lot of thought to the responsibility that goes along with having them. I watched people I knew get married and have kids, and how their lives changed suddenly and dramatically. I saw parenting as a tremendous responsibility. I admire people who parent and who do it well. I just couldn't see myself ever doing it.

But it's real tough to opt out of it. To make the choice not to have them takes more courage than to have them like everybody else. Having children is something we're "supposed to do," but when I was honest with myself, it was something I didn't want.

*It's widely held that women have children because they are fulfilling a natural biological urge. What do you think about this?*

Carole: I think women have a biological urge. My biological clock was definitely going off, and Rich kept hitting the snooze alarm until I just didn't need the clock anymore!

Rich: I don't think there is an urge with men. When it comes to having children, a lot of men do what their wives want them to do. Although they may feel it, no man in his right mind would ever say they don't want or like kids. The idea that "I'm a man" because I have a son or daughter still really exists today—it is not just a machismo

*Laura Carroll*

cultural thing. For a man, if there is an urge, it is probably part of the desire to leave a legacy. They want to be remembered.

*Is there anything about you or your background that you think might have influenced you not to want children?*

Rich: When I was growing up, I saw the tremendous responsibility that my parents carried. I had two older brothers, and money was always tight. My parents worked hard; my father worked at a steel company, and my mother sewed in a factory.

My father was an alcoholic, and died at forty-four. He wasn't a mean drunk, but when he drank, my parents argued. I worried about whether I would be a parent—could I be a lot of what my father wasn't?

Carole: I know Rich would have been a good father. I have seen him with children—all of his gentle, wonderful qualities are exactly the sort of things that make a good father. He has a gentle voice and gets on their level. They love his fuzzy face and just hook right into him.

Rich: Kids scare the hell out of me. I have to watch myself with kids. I have to be more careful with everything I say and do.

Carole: For many years I worshipped in the Lutheran church, and I have a strong relationship with God. The day of my epiphany, God spoke to me. I think of myself as someone who wanted children, but my epiphany made me see that I had a choice to have them or not.

*What has been toughest about not having kids?*

Rich: It is easy to feel like an outcast when you don't belong to the biggest club in the world.

Carole: We don't fit into the milieu. Most of my siblings and relatives have kids, and get together and talk about things that I have no clue about. For the kids' sake, I am interested in things like soccer, but it is not my world. I often don't feel my relatives who are parents are interested in my world. They are so busy with theirs.

It also felt tough not to give grandchildren to my parents. My mother had always said that when my brother's wife and I gave her a grandchild, we would get diamond earrings. My sister-in-law got diamond earrings when my niece was born. The following Christmas my parents gave me diamond earrings. It felt so special that, even though they wanted grandchildren, they accepted me and my choice.

*Do you have any regrets about not having children?*

Rich: I think I may only have regrets when I am old, in a nursing home, and no one comes to see me.

*Laura Carroll*

Carole: This is why we are being very nice to our nieces and nephews!

Rich: I think I'll always wonder what it would have been like. What exactly did I miss?—but in the end, I wasn't curious enough to find out.

*Let's say a couple who is trying to decide whether they want children is asking your advice. What advice would you give to help them make their decision?*

Carole: I would tell them not to talk so much about the baby, but to talk about and focus on each other to find out who they really are, as individuals and as a couple. Then overlay baby and parenting on top of that. If couples don't do that, what is the parenting going to be founded on?

Rich: I would ask them to talk to people who have children, and get beyond all of the hundreds of positive things they will say. I really think parents are afraid to admit how hard it is and how many times they wish they didn't have the responsibility. People are seen as ogres if they admit that parenthood is not all roses, and that it's tough.

Carole: Parents may feel disloyal if they admit it is not all roses.

*What impressions do you think others have of you, as a couple that has chosen not to have children?*

Carole: People commonly see childfree men and women as self-ish. The way I see it, if they see us as selfish, they get to see themselves as self*less*—and that's supposed to be a good thing.

Rich: I often get the message from others that, because we don't have children, we don't have a right to voice our opinions about kids. I can't tell you how many times I have heard, "You don't know; you don't have kids." I think to myself, "I may not have kids, but I do know some things about them." I *was* a kid once myself.

Carole: People have made comments that seem to assume that we don't like children. It's wrong. It has nothing to do with liking or loving kids. Some people who choose not to have children don't like them. Others adore them. We just chose not to have them in our lives full-time. I know me, and I know that I can offer the best of me to the kids in my life, as their aunt and godmother.

Overall, I have to say that since I started putting my decision out there as a positive thing, people get the positive spin and are less likely to make negative insinuations. The attitude I project deflects it.

*How, if at all, do you perceive yourselves as different from people who have children?*

Carole: I think I have a much better sense of self—of who I am, than someone who is being someone else's mom. I've gotten to explore myself and let my life play out in a lot of different directions.

Rich: I watch a lot of parents become "grown ups" and begin to let the real them come out only on rare occasions, usually when they are drinking! I have never had to do that. When I look in the mirror, I don't see a fifty-one year old person. I see me. The only time I feel old is when I see somebody I went to high school with who looks old.

Carole: I agree! We seem younger.

Rich: Having kids makes you grow up real fast.

Carole: Growing older is required; growing up is an option!

*What do you see as your role in molding the next generation of children?*

Rich: Our niece and godson are our main focus.

Carole: I want to be a safe place they can always come to, and help give them avenues to express who they are. I want to help them feel valued. Whether we're parents, aunts, uncles, or just people on the street—everyone can do this for children.

*Tell me how your love story began.*

Carole: We met at a seminar on finding fulfillment in life. After dating for about a year and a half, we got engaged, and then got married eight months later.

Rich: I just couldn't see myself spending the rest of my life without this wonderful person.

*What kind of time do you spend together?*

Carole: We don't spend enough time together. I am a night owl. He has to get up early. I am social and like to go out more than Rich does. We spend Mondays and lots of evenings together. He has Mondays off, and I try to take them off so we can be together.

Rich: We have been involved in local theater. I have been in plays, and serve on the theater board. Carole has been in plays and does the theater's newsletter.

Carole: Rich may be introverted, but he is so good on stage!

*What is your circle of friends like?*

Carole: I cultivate my friendships with people from a variety of backgrounds. I always used to think Rich and I had to do everything together. I would either stay home, or drag him out, kicking and screaming. That has shifted over the years. I do what I need to do and say, "You're welcome to come." Sometimes, he does; sometimes, he doesn't. Sometimes it takes me away from home a bit more often than I would like, and I feel torn. I want to be involved with my friends, and I also want to be with Rich.

Rich: Keeping up with her and her friends' energy is a lot of work for me!

*How do you handle various aspects of the day-to-day things in marriage, for example, domestics and money management?*

Carole: If somebody cooks, it is usually me. We mostly cook "easy" meals, and pop things in the microwave. I eat out a lot with friends.

If the cleaning happens, it is me. He takes the lead on the laundry. Dishes—me. Shopping for food—him.

Rich: We have always kept two accounts. We mostly divide up the essentials.

*Tell me about your relationship with your pets.*

Carole: I have had cats for many years. The four we have now are our children in fur coats! We are very attached to them. Sometimes, I think Rich talks more to them than to me!

Rich: Cats were my first pets, and after a bit of adjusting, I definitely became a "cat person."

*What have been your biggest marital challenges?*

Carole: Several years into our marriage, we took some time apart. We were struggling with our personality differences and the child issue. I was in college studying theater, and left for four months to do a semester in London. We learned what it was like to live separately and decided we didn't want to. The time away didn't change my feeling about having kids then, but it clarified many feelings I had about our relationship.

Our styles are so different; being in a relationship with someone who is my polar opposite has been a lot of work. One of the biggest things I have had to learn is when I put something out there to Rich, I can't expect a response from him right away. I have to put it out there, and walk away. Emotionally I am like a microwave, and he is a crock-pot! I just have to put him on slow cook! I have to shut up and back off.

Rich: I need time to think about things. I am also very quiet. When I come home from work, I don't want to be alone. I like to watch television, and enjoy doing it with Carole.

Carole: He won't want to talk much as we watch television, but

he'll want me to be there with him. This is hard for me. I am the type who wants to talk during the commercials!

*In your experience, what are the ingredients to making marriage work over the long term?*

Rich: Communication. If I don't express myself, it gets me into trouble. I also have to stay in the moment, really listen to Carole, and not get distracted with thoughts in my own head.

Carole: Two people have to open their hearts, and really let the other person in. Rich was the first man I allowed myself to do this with.

It is also important to reflect back to the other person what you hear him/her say, and who you see him/her to be. One partner will see things that the other person just won't recognize in themselves. It's a gift one person can give to another. Most of the time, it's the good things that we see, but sometimes we see things that aren't working, and we have to be brave enough to say, "Honey, this isn't working for you."

*How does society view the institution of marriage today?*

Carole: I think more and more married people today see marriage as less about procreation, and more about a connection with someone on an intimate level that they choose not to have with anyone else.

Rich: The institution of marriage is the ultimate commitment to this intimate connection.

Carole: We have had rough times. It would have been much easier to call it quits, but the promise we made when we got married carries weight, and the love and commitment carry even greater weight.

By holding up a good marriage, we can be an example of these values in action.

# DIANNE AND WOLFGANG

*I realized that I was more in love with the idea of having*
*children than what it really means to have them.*
*-Dianne*

$\mathcal{D}$ ianne and Wolfgang have been married twenty-three years. They both grew up in Tennessee, and met in high school. After a career in mechanical engineering, Wolfgang started a blacksmith business called Wolfgang Forge. Dianne helps him with the business and cares for children part-time.

We met on a sunny Sunday afternoon. Wolfgang had to check out a forge project in my neighborhood, so afterwards, we met in my home. Dianne and Wolfgang filled our conversation with their southern charm. As we talked, their dogs panted at my screen door and looked loyally at their masters.

~

*How did you decide that you did not want children?*

Dianne: I had always planned to have children, but initially made my decision not to have them because Wolfgang didn't want them.

Wolfgang decided a long time ago that he did not want children. Before we were married, I held out hope that he would change his mind. Once we were married, it was clear his mind was made up. He had a vasectomy right quick.

I began to change my own mind when I began babysitting. It was a good trial run to see what it would have been like to raise children. Because of babysitting, I now know I do not want children! I have learned I don't have a lot of patience for children. A person has to be more sociable when she/he has children, and I am not a sociable person.

I am happier now with the decision we made not to have them. I realized that I was more in love with the idea of having children than what it really means to have them.

If we had kids, I think we'd be divorced. We have more disagree-ments on how to discipline our dog, Igor, than everything else com-bined! Also, we barely have time for us as it is. People are often so harried, with no time for themselves. Having children makes it harder to find time for each other.

Wolfgang: I was young when I knew I did not want them. I was the oldest of three children and got a taste of parenting early on because I baby-sat my siblings a lot. I didn't like kids even as a kid. I always wanted to hang around with the older kids.

As an adult, I knew that I was unwilling to give up so much of my time for something I really did not like. Even if I had wanted them, having children would have limited me. I started my career as an industrial mechanic and machinist, and it took me to many places. By the time I was twenty-eight, I had topped out in my field. After much deliberation, I decided to go back to college and get my mechanical engineering degree. I could not have done this if I had had children.

*Do you have any regrets about not having children?*

Dianne: I only regret that I won't have someone to think of me as I think of my mother.

Wolfgang: I don't really care about continuing my lineage. There are a number of people on both sides of my family who are terminally strange!

*Let's say a couple who is trying to decide whether they want children is asking your advice. What advice would you give to help them make their decision?*

Dianne: I would tell them to baby sit a group of at least three children of varied ages for at least a week. I think it can be an eye-opening experience to the twenty-four-hour nature of children be-fore deciding to have them.

*Laura Carroll*

Wolfgang: I would advise them to consider it seriously, don't rush the decision, and don't fall for the common notion, "because we *can* have kids, we *should* have kids." I would remind them that we have the capacity to rise above our genes, and it is perfectly fine to do so.

If the couple decided they wanted children, I would encourage them not to rule out adoption. There are so many kids out there that need a whole lot of love, and we have far too many people on this planet as it is.

*What perceptions do you think other people have of you, as a couple that has chosen not to have children?*

Wolfgang: I believe they think my motives are selfish, and they are. My wife is the most important thing in my life, and I don't want to divide her up with anything else. She's it. She's all. I wouldn't want to dilute what we have in any way.

Dianne: They probably think we aren't in step with the trends today! It is such a child-oriented society. For a while, yuppies weren't having kids; then all of the sudden they had them, and now everything seems to cater to kids.

*Based on your experience, what are society's assumptions and misconceptions about married couples who consciously choose not to parent?*

Wolfgang: Society sends us the message that if we're against doing everything in the world for kids, there is something wrong with us. Even our tax system encourages people to have kids. I'd like this to change. If a person wants to have a child, I don't want to have to pay for it. I don't have the right to tell others what to do/not to do, but I feel I do have a say when I have to pay for it. I see it as a legally enforceable type of prejudice against people who cannot have, or do not want, children.

*How did your love story begin?*

Dianne: I knew we were meant to be together from the moment I met Wolfgang. I pursued him, but at first he didn't like me.

Wolfgang: I finally came around. We dated for three years, during which time we broke up several times, but she found all my hiding places!

I came to the slow realization that I'll never find anyone better than Dianne. She is so kind and understanding. This lady has my best interests at heart more than I do! I can't imagine anyone who would be better for me.

*Many couples get married when they're ready to start a family. This wasn't the case for you. Why did you get married?*

Wolfgang: At the time, I had just accepted a job in Germany, and we got married one week before my departure.

Dianne: He decided to marry me because wives could go to Germany for free!

Wolfgang: I was going to marry her sooner or later, and I thought if I marry her now, I will save a $1,200 ticket—Mr. Romance, huh?!

Seriously, I married Dianne because I don't have a lot of friends, nor do I want a lot of friends. I wanted one person I could be very close with.

Dianne: I respect the institution of marriage. If two people are committed to each other, you get married. It is just what you do. I am Christian and believe that God has set it up this way.

Wolfgang: To me, living together seems cowardly. It's easier to break up. I decided early on that if were going to marry, I was going to do it only one time.

*What is your life together like?*

Wolfgang: The forging business takes up a big part of our lives.

Dianne: Outside of work, we have a quiet life. Mostly, we just like being together. We like a lot of physical contact, even if it's just sitting on the sofa, holding hands.

Wolfgang: We love to walk the dogs, and cook together. Dianne and I don't go out of our way to be social. We like to be with each other so much that we don't have much need to be with other people. Some people think we're more weird because we're like this than because we don't have kids, but there is no one on the planet I want to be with more than Dianne.

*Laura Carroll*

*Tell me about your relationship with your dogs.*

Dianne: They *are* our kids. People make fun of us, but we just love our animals. I love their unconditional love, and that they are good guard dogs.

Wolfgang: I agree with Dianne; they are our kids. I am sure I love them more than I could ever love human children. I spend quite a bit of time training them to make sure they mind and don't endanger other people.

*What do you see as your role in molding the next generation of children?*

Wolfgang: A willingness to be a role model and to help educate them. I help the neighborhood children, by teaching them to forge and helping them on math and other school projects.

Dianne: I care for and help children every time I baby-sit.

*What have been some of your marital challenges?*

Wolfgang: Dianne's father raised her in a traditional, patriarchal fashion and brought her up to be wholly dependent. However, Dianne has always been strong-willed, just quiet about it. We have worked on overcoming her upbringing, so she can be more independent and our relationship can feel more like a partnership.

Dianne: Also, at first, I was jealous in our marriage. I didn't feel that attractive.

Wolfgang: I helped Dianne get over this by aggravating the dickens out of her! I tried to tease her lovingly until she realized I was doing it just to rile her, and saw how ridiculous the jealousy was!

Dianne: Wolfgang has been the jealous one when I spend a lot of time with other people on our trips home to Tennessee. Over the years, going home to see family has created stress. When we visit, Wolfgang just wants to sit in his parents' home. I want to go everywhere and see everyone. We worked it out; he goes back home for a few days, and I just stay longer!

*What are the ingredients to making it work over the long term?*

Wolfgang: Each of us has the other's happiness foremost in our minds. When only one person has this idea, it is not a good thing. I am happiest when she is happy.

It takes being more concerned with the other person's happiness than your own. Even if it's not what you feel like doing or want to do at that moment, put making your spouse happy first. We both try to be worth this sort of attention.

Dianne: Be sweet. Help the other person keep a perspective of him/herself. Others may think Wolfgang is being mean when he teases me, but he does it in such a way that it makes me laugh at myself. It always has a kernel of truth in it. He helps me not take myself so seriously.

It also takes spending time together. There is a lot of talk about quality time with kids, but not much talk about quality time with your spouse. Your spouse is most important, and you need to give him/her some time. She or he deserves it.

Couples also need to be able to communicate more openly and tell the truth more, even if it is hard to.

Wolfgang: In society in general, too many people have come to treat the truth as a relative term.

Dianne: People even lie as part of everyday conversation these days.

Wolfgang: People focus so heavily on saying the right thing and looking good. This needs to be stripped away, especially with the one you love.

Dianne: In the end, you can only be happy in marriage if you are happy with, and can live with, yourself. If you lie to others and to yourself, how can you possibly be happy?

*Laura Carroll*

*How, if at all, would you change the institution of marriage today?*

Dianne: For a better future, I would not change the institution of marriage as much as I would change how couples raise their children. I think people are too liberal in how they raise kids today. Parents often reward bad behavior. Children are so materialistic. Parents give their children too much and don't expect anything of them, like chores. Children are robbed of learning how to appreciate things

when they are brought up, being given so many things. So often, they don't see that gifts are special.

Wolfgang: I would like to see being faithful as more than when people feel like it. So many marriages are like this. The thought of Dianne losing her trust in me would be one of the most painful things in my life.

# ERIN AND JEFF

After five years into our marriage,
we finally asked ourselves,
"Why *do* people have kids?"

-Jeff

*E*rin and Jeff have been married for twelve years. Erin grew up in Portland, Oregon, and Jeff is from Chicago. They met in college. Erin teaches middle school, and Jeff teaches high school.

When I arrived at their home, Erin and Jeff were eating Chinese takeout, and invited me to join them. Surrounded by a lovely custom wood interior and mantles lined with family pictures, we sat in their dining room and ate while we talked. Their two playful cats made their presence known, from purrs to a bit of mischief.

~

*How did you decide that you did not want children?*

Erin: Before I was married, I definitely thought I would have kids. I am a good Catholic girl!

Jeff: I always thought I'd have kids, and I was raised a good Catholic kid too. In high school and college, I wasn't much of a free thinker. My parents had a big influence on what I was going to do with my life.

We got married a year after we got out of college and knew we didn't want kids right away. We planned to start a family in three years, but when the time came, we had no burning desire. We were both working and enjoying being together. We decided to wait a little longer. After five years into our marriage, we finally asked ourselves, "Why *do* people have kids?" Our lives were very full!

Erin: It remains fairly uncommon for people to be open about consciously choosing not to have children. About two years into our marriage, we met a couple who had made this choice. They were the first people we had encountered who talked openly about choosing not to have children.

Jeff: Up until that point, I had not been exposed to this lifestyle. My decision came as part of maturing and seeing the world from other than through my parents.

Erin: Through our work and families, we had a good idea of what we'd be in for as parents.

Jeff: We each work with 160 kids a day. We also have nieces, nephews, and friends with kids.

Erin: I know why people have kids; they are wonderful, and they bring lots of joy. I love kids, but I am so tired by the time I get home from work that I can't imagine trying to expend energy for two relationships—husband and children.

*What is the biggest reason that you decided not to have kids?*

Erin: I realized I didn't really, really want to have kids. I like to come home and have time to myself. Teaching middle school is really hard work. It's loud, chaotic, and stressful, and I can only take this for so long. Many people do a great job of being parents and teaching. I don't think I am one of them.

Jeff: I never woke up and said, "I'd love to be a dad." I didn't feel I had any business being a parent unless I felt this way.

*Is there anything about you or your background that you think might have influenced you not to want children?*

Erin: In many ways, I had the Cleaver family. I have two brothers and a sister, and I am the oldest and the bossiest. I was raised to be driven and to always have a lot going on. I am not sure if these are the best attributes for having kids.

Jeff: My dad is an alcoholic, and my childhood wasn't always a happy one. I didn't really realize this until I no longer lived at home. My dad didn't always model being a good father. He and his dad also had a terrible relationship. I know the textbook version of fatherhood, and I can be a "good dad" at school with my students, but when push comes to shove around the house, I don't know how good of a father I would have been.

If you look in a co-dependency manual, you'll see my family. Even if it's way in the back of my mind, this is one of the reasons I don't want kids. I'm not sure that I could overcome "doing what I know."

*Laura Carroll*

*Do you have any regrets about not having children?*

Erin: Sometimes. I see how my nephew runs up to my brother, shouting "Daddy, Daddy!" It's something very special we will never have, but it doesn't compel me to have a child.

Jeff: I don't have any regrets. I can't picture myself living twenty-four hours a day with kids around.

Erin: I think about the regrets I may have had if I would have *had* kids. I know older people who didn't do things they wanted to do because they were taking care of their family. They look back and regret what they didn't do with their lives.

*Let's say a couple who is trying to decide whether they want children is asking your advice. What advice would you give to help them make their decision?*

Jeff: I would tell them to write down a list of what they will gain and lose if they have kids. Then I'd tell them to look at the things at the top of the list and ask how many of the gains are about "me, me, me." Having kids is more about the kids and the family, than about one's self.

If "someone to pass on my family heirlooms to" appears on the list, I would encourage them to rethink it. This was one of my big concerns about not having kids at first. I'll have all of this family memorabilia, and I asked myself, "Who am I going to give it to?" If my younger brother doesn't have kids, it's the end of my family line. Then I realized what a ridiculous reason this is to have children. Passing on all of this stuff is like carving your name into a national monument to prove that you were there. In the big scheme of things, what does it matter if someone has a box of photos that she/he hasn't looked at in fifty years?

Erin: I'd encourage them to try rental children first. There is nothing like hanging out with them for long periods of time to get a feel for what it's like.

Jeff: I'd tell them to wait until they wake up and say, "I want to have kids," and not to do it until then.

*Have you experienced less than positive judgments from others because you don't have kids?*

Jeff: We've experienced little guilt trips. Some friends have said things like "You're traveling again? Oh, that's right, you don't have kids." It also seems that they feel a bit jealous, that they are thinking to themselves, "I wish we could do that."

Society expects people to have kids, and if you don't, you're odd. People make judgments because they are trying to figure out the reason why others are different, and often "because they're selfish" comes up as the reason.

I think my mom might harbor this one. We're not giving her the chance to be a grandmother.

We don't think that we're selfish. Many people *have* kids out of pure selfish reasons—they "had two girls, and really want a boy," so they have a third child.

*Laura Carroll*

*Why is that selfish?*

Jeff: Because it's "I want, I want." It's a very egocentric reason. So is "I want to carry on the family name." It is a short-term decision with long-term impacts.

Erin: So is not thinking about how many people are on the planet already, and how the resources are running out in a big hurry.

Jeff: I think it is irresponsible to have more than two children in this day and age.

Erin: More than judgments, mostly I think that people just don't understand us. They can't imagine not having kids. They must think we're weird, or think that we can't have kids.

Jeff: Some people probably don't believe us when we tell them we don't want kids. People can't accept it, so they think we just haven't gotten to that point yet. They think that maybe we just need a little encouraging, and that someday we'll figure it out.

*Based on your experience, what are society's assumptions or misconceptions about people who consciously choose not to parent?*

Jeff: I think society often assumes that women who do not have children must be "career women." They think Erin must want to devote more time to her career.

Erin: I think society accepts women who say they want a career instead of children more than women who don't have children but who also don't say they want to focus on a career. People seem to need a <u>reason</u> from those of us who don't want children; yet, it is almost unheard of to ask a woman why she <u>had</u> a child.

*How, if at all, do you see yourselves as different from those who have children?*

Erin: I think we take more time to think about things than many people do. Both of us are probably more high strung than most. When you have children, you have to be able to be less like this; you have to be able to go with the flow.

*What do you see as your role in molding the next generation of children?*

Erin: We all have a responsibility to create our society. We all have responsibilities to make ourselves important in the lives of at least "a" child. For me this means playing an important role in my nieces' and nephews' lives. Children are the next generation and the ones who will be caring for us.

Jeff: And they are the next generation of parents! It is so important to model a healthy relationship. A lot of kids don't get to see a healthy marriage.

Erin: We need to model making thoughtful choices. Kids need to see different aspects of a relationship. I never saw my parents fight, and I didn't have good conflict resolution skills when I got into our relationship.

I also want to model living outside traditional gender roles. For example, I like to cook with my nephews because it is commonly seen as a "girl" thing.

Jeff: I have connected with some students above and beyond the classroom. One student came from a dysfunctional family, which rang all kinds of bells for me. We still keep in touch. I'm a sounding board for her. A lot of these kids are just screaming for someone to listen to them.

*How did your love story begin?*

Jeff: We met during our last year in college. We just clicked, and spent almost every waking moment together. We dated for a year, got engaged, and a year later, got married.

Erin: We worked at the same school during the first two years we were married. We had the same schedule every day, and had the same

*Laura Carroll*

colleagues and friends. It was actually the perfect way to start the marriage. We had a lot of time to spend together, and it was a completely shared experience.

Jeff: It solidified our marriage. I have to admit we got lucky. We got married so young, and it's worked out.

Erin: Think how much we have changed. Imagine if we hadn't changed in the same ways!

Jeff: We could have gone in completely different directions.

*What kind of time do you spend together?*

Jeff: Almost all of our non-working hours are spent together. We're homebodies. We sometimes go out for dinner and like to go out for ice cream! We spend time with friends at least once a week on the weekends. We also regularly spend time with Erin's family.

Erin: Sometimes, we'll both be at home, but doing our own thing. I like to do crafts, and Jeff plays on the computer.

We like to travel and like to plan the travel. Planning is half the fun! We go to the library, and get a stack of books on our destination. We've been to Europe twice, the Virgin Islands three times, and all around the U.S. and Mexico.

Jeff: We usually take three to four trips a year. We went to Europe for eight weeks; as teachers, we get the summers off! We go on at least one trip each year during the summer and spring vacations.

*How do you handle various aspects of the day-to-day things in marriage, for example, domestics and money management?*

Erin: Jeff does all the money stuff because I don't like doing it. I love to cook, so I do most of the cooking. He cleans up.

Jeff: You probably do more laundry than I do.

Erin: But we split most other things. We share the ironing because, believe it or not, we both like doing it.

*Laura Carroll*

*What is your circle of friends like?*

Erin: We're at an age when a lot of our friends are having kids. These days we're trying to find friends who don't have kids, not because we don't like our friends with children anymore, but because I don't feel I should be calling them to do things like before. They should be spending time with their kids. I know how special that time is, how expensive babysitters are, and how tricky it is to get it all to work.

Jeff: Then there's the situation where we call a couple and ask them to come over and do x, and we mean just <u>them</u>. We're in the position of having to say "without your kids," or hoping that they understand this. Either way, we're putting the burden on them, expecting them to get a babysitter.

Erin: It's rather awkward.

Jeff: We've drifted away from some friends because they have had kids. It is unfortunate, but a reality.

*Tell me about your relationship with your pets.*

Erin: Some people say pets are their surrogate children. This is not true for us.

Jeff: They are fun, low maintenance, and we enjoy their affection.

*What have been your biggest marital challenges?*

Erin: Money. We've never been poor; we've always had jobs, but sometimes money has gotten tight, like when we remodeled our house.

*What has been important to working things out?*

Erin: When tension has existed between us, it's felt uncomfortable, but we have never let it go for more than a few hours.

Jeff: We say what we think and feel. We don't hold back. I have <u>learned</u> to be this way—it wasn't like this in my house growing up. Erin has helped me learn to be more open. It's a real strength in our marriage.

*What are the ingredients to making it work over the long term?*

Erin: Being openly affectionate. Say lots of "I love you's," and have lots of hand holding and kissing. Touch is so important. The more we get it at home, the better off we'll be.

Jeff: We use the "90/10" rule when we get into a fight. We ask ourselves if the issue falls into the 90% category of those that really don't matter, or if it's in the 10% of those that do. Is it worth focusing our time on it? Do we want it to consume our entire evening? Most of the time, it is not something that has to be made into a big issue.

*In your opinion, how does society view the institution of marriage today?*

Jeff: It is a minority, but there are a growing number of people in our society that don't put pregnancy and marriage together.

Erin: I think marriage is sacred and an important commitment. It seems that many people in our society don't see it this way, given high divorce rates. It is important to me that people know I have made this commitment, and that I am proud to be married to Jeff.

Jeff: Marriage is more of an external than an internal thing. *I* know I have made this commitment to Erin, but I think that even if we lived together for fifty years, society would question our commitment to each other. Even if we have the strongest relationship there is, marriage is expected of a couple.

*Laura Carroll*

Erin: I think we were like most people—we got married because "that's what you do" when you're in love and have a strong bond.

Jeff: Now we have this <u>incredible</u> bond. I don't need to wear my ring to prove it. On the other hand, I am proud to wear this ring. I want people to know I'm married to an incredible person.

# NANCY AND DAN

Even if people have political, social, or intellectual reasons
not to have children, having kids comes down to an
emotional decision.

-Dan

*N*ancy and Dan were married in 1987. She is originally from
Baltimore, and Dan grew up in Bethesda, Maryland. They
each own their own business. Nancy is an architect and graphic
designer, and Dan owns Jump Jump, a music mail order LP record
company. They met through a mutual friend.

We met on a fall evening. When I arrived, Nancy and Dan were
preparing a ravioli dinner. We ate a delicious meal as we talked.

~

*How did you decide that you did not want children?*

Nancy: I have never had a burning desire to have children. By the
age of thirty-seven, I felt sure I did not want to be a mother.

Dan: Before I met Nancy, I was never in a relationship that was
serious enough for the subject of children to come up. I affirmed my
decision about children when Nancy and I discussed the issue
before we were married. I hadn't mapped out any of my life until then.
The only thing I knew I wanted to do was own a record store one day.

*What are the biggest reasons that you decided you did not want children?*

Nancy: I simply did not have the desire to have children. It was purely an emotional decision.

Dan: I don't think I would be up for the responsibility, and I don't want interference with my lifestyle. Most importantly, I never felt emotionally drawn to have children—I never had a real desire.

I think people who have children do it out of real desire. Even if people have political, social, or intellectual reasons not to have children, having kids comes down to an emotional decision.

Each person's choice on children, and how many they have, is a personal choice and has nothing to do with larger issues. Ultimately, I don't think you can make the political be personal.

*So the emotional overrules the intellectual/political/social?*

Dan: I think that many people have the desire and just do it.

Nancy: Maybe intellectual, political, and social issues are reasons for some people who do not have children, but they are not reasons for me.

Dan: I just think it boils down to whether a person has that personal, emotional desire.

*Is there anything that feels tough about not having kids?*

Dan: There is nothing hard about it. I don't feel pressure from our family, friends, or society to have children.

Nancy: Our friends and families know and respect the fact that we don't want children. They understand it without having to question us.

*Let's say a couple who is trying to decide whether they want children is asking your advice. What advice would you give to help them make their decision?*

Nancy: Follow your heart.

*Laura Carroll*

Dan: I saw an article in the newspaper recently called, "Are You

Ready for Children?" It had a quiz, and said things like, "to see if you're ready, set your alarm for every two hours throughout the night, get up, and walk around with a big bag of sugar for forty-five minutes!" I don't think we can ask ourselves things like, "Do you want sleep deprivation, dirty diapers, or to deal with teenagers?" We have to listen to what is inside us.

*What impressions do you think others have of you, as a couple that has chosen not to have children?*

Nancy: I think they think we are very happy.

Dan: I think they think we have a lot of free time and disposable income.

*Based on your experience, what are society's assumptions and misconceptions about married couples who consciously choose not to parent?*

Dan: I think society must have changed from the days when people assume couples would have children. I have never felt any pressure, or anything negative, so I am guessing that society has become much more accepting of how people choose to live their lives.

*What do you see as your role in molding the next generation of children?*

Nancy: Just try to be a good role model to everyone I encounter.

Dan: That's what I think—we set an example with how we live our lives. Kids often lack examples of people living ethical and honest lives. Even the smallest things set an example, like kids seeing us pick up litter at the park.

*How did your love story begin?*

Nancy: Dan was living in Seattle, where I had decided to go to architectural school. A friend of mine who knew Dan gave me his name. I called him, and we had dinner at his house and hit it off right away. About five months after we met, I was deeply in love.

Dan: We were together about eight months before marriage became imminent. After about five months, we moved in together and, shortly after, stated our desire to spend the rest of our lives together. We made it public and got married about a year and a half after that.

*Laura Carroll*

*Many couples get married when they're ready to start a family. This wasn't the case for you. Why did you get married?*

Dan: We first decided we wanted to spend our lives together. Then we decided we wanted to make this commitment public. We wanted to share our commitment with our family and friends.

Marriage gave a sense of security to the relationship. Once we were married, my relationship with Nancy's parents changed over night. It became less formal. I became part of the family and less of a guest. I also think Nancy's parents no longer feared I would distract her from architecture school and threaten her future.

Marriage changed my relationship with family as well. I remember my father saying to me, "I thought you were one of those people who was always going to be a kid." I think, in his eyes, the fact I entered into a marriage made me an adult.

*What is your life together like?*

Dan: For the last four years, we have both worked out of this house. My store sits at the front of the house, and Nancy's office is in the rear of the house.

Nancy: Our day-to-day life has a steady rhythm. We always have breakfast together. Then we go to work and try to meet up to walk the dog together in the park twice a day.

Our social life mostly consists of playing the card game "500" once a week with a group of friends. We have a close circle of friends who meet for dinner every other week. We also share the holidays.

We like to take in an occasional movie and, in the summer, work in the garden and sit outside in the evenings.

Dan: We both like to read, and talk to each other about what we're reading.

0-CARR

*How do you handle various aspects of the day-to-day things in marriage, for
example, domestics and money management?*

Nancy: We each share in what needs to be done. We try to work
together.

*Tell me about your relationship with your pets.*

Dan: They are part of our family.
Nancy: I love my dog and cat. My dog, in particular, is central to
my life.

*What do you think are the ingredients to making marriage work over the long term?*

Nancy: At my parents' fiftieth wedding anniversary celebration,
we asked them this question, and two of the most important things I
recall were being a team, and not having to get your way.
Dan: We're both easy-going, rarely fight, and haven't really had

*Laura Carroll*

challenging times. I think the reason is that we can let go and don't get too frustrated by things. We don't let things become an issue.

Nancy: A big ingredient is feeling good about yourself—feeling confident, healthy, and comfortable with yourself.

Dan: We have very separate work lives, and we have to make sure we make time to be together. A routine and regular contact are key to making it work.

*In your opinion, how does society view the institution of marriage today?*

Nancy: Not as very sacred.

Dan: The institution of marriage is no longer the second step in a relationship after "going steady." In the 1970's, people used negative terms like, "living in sin," or "shacking up." Now people more likely say, "My daughter is living with her boyfriend." It's no big deal.

*Would you like to see this change?*

Dan: I like the public declaration of a person's commitment to the relationship and to the other person. To me, it makes it a real commitment, and it's a wonderful, romantic thing. A lot of people living together have not made this kind of commitment. I hope that everyone finds the person they want to make this kind of commitment with.

*Laura Carroll*

# AMY AND PETE

Too often, having a child is the easy answer
to a life without clear direction.

-Amy

*A*my and Pete have been married for seventeen years. Amy is from Ohio, and Pete grew up in Michigan. Pete was Amy's neighbor when she moved to Oregon.

Although they are in their forties, Amy and Pete live a semi-retired lifestyle. For over twenty-three years, Pete worked as a corporate pilot. For the last four years, he has taken a break from this work and has spent more of his time managing their investments. Amy has worked in retail and, these days, when they are not traveling, works part-time in the travel industry. Amy, Pete, and their cat live half of the year on their boat in the Bahamas.

Unfortunately, we did not meet on their boat in the tropical sun! I interviewed them in their bright, contemporary home. We sat on a cozy white sofa, and had iced coffee and homemade cookies.

~

*How did you decide that you did not want children?*

Amy: I am the oldest of five in my family, and got my share of taking care of children when I was growing up. I have never felt comfortable around babies. Even if Pete and I would have had the desire, until the last few years, Pete traveled extensively and was home only ten days a month. I would not have wanted full responsibility for a child when he was away so much.

Pete: We decided early on in our marriage we did not want to have children. I just never had the desire. When I'm honest with myself, I don't think I would be a good parent. I don't have the patience it takes to nurture the way a person needs to when raising children. I also think that, though we're both in our forties, we don't feel like "grown ups!" We are having so much fun together and don't want to put off the things we want to do now.

*It's widely held that women have children because they are fulfilling a natural biological urge. What do you think about this?*

Amy: When my sister called to tell me she had her baby, I couldn't sleep that night. I think women have a built-in maternal urge, and we can't deny it, but the big thing is whether a person wants to fulfill it or not. I have felt it but have never wanted to act on it.

*Is there anything about you or your background that might have influenced you not to want children?*

Amy: Growing up, I was the designated babysitter. As cousins started having kids and I was always the sitter, it started to bother me, especially when I was in charge of newborns. It was scary! I never felt comfortable.

My parents had their share of fighting, as everyone does, but I never saw them as a loving couple until after we'd grown up and left the house. We weren't rich by any means, but my parents took vacations without us, and left us with mean babysitters.

My mom was also out a lot, doing whatever women did in the sixties. I never felt close to her. I actually felt closer to a cleaning woman that we had for years. The day JFK was shot, we watched television and cried together.

Pete: My parents were regimented and serious. Our family environment felt more formal than openly warm or affectionate. My father was a chemistry professor, and in many ways, he treated me like a student. It benefited me in school and led to my technology interests as I got older. When I was a kid, I went with him on his business travels

*Families of Two* ∴ *177* ∾

around the world. I think this instilled the traveler in me, which is not the sort of lifestyle for a parent.

Amy: We both have nomadic histories. This is the longest place I have lived anywhere, and we have only lived here four years. We both love the feeling of being on the move. For us, it is more fun to be on the road than at home. It's not a lifestyle that's set up for children.

*Let's say a couple who is trying to decide whether they want children is asking your advice. What advice would you give to help them make their decision?*

Amy: I have found my best friend and lover for life, and I don't know if children would have enhanced our relationship. I would tell couples to think about whether they want their relationship to change, and change dramatically, because it will when children enter the picture. Couples need to believe having children will change their relationship in a positive way.

Pete: I would tell them, "Don't be afraid not to have children." If the word "should" enters into their thinking at all, I would advise them to think harder about what they really want to do with their lives.

Amy: If one or both of them weren't sure about what they wanted to do with their lives, or felt something was missing, I would encourage them to find the answer to these questions before having a child. Too often, having a child is the easy answer to a life without clear direction.

*What perceptions do you think others have of you, as a couple who has chosen not to have children?*

Pete: More than anything, I think others are jealous of us, especially now with the boat. Older people we encounter in the Bahamas encourage and compliment us. They say things to us like, "Good for you that you're doing this now. We wish we would have done it sooner!"

*Based on your experience, what are society's assumptions and misconceptions about married couples who consciously choose not to parent?*

Pete: It's changing. There are so many lifestyles out there now, that I think society is more accepting of couples like us.

Amy: I agree; it's definitely changing. It's no longer strange not to have children. You know it's no longer so weird when Ann Landers takes it on in her column and advises readers to weigh the pros and cons, and not to have them because they think they should.

*Do you perceive yourselves as different from the general population?*

Pete: Maybe we're somewhat different from the norm because we don't have children, but I think we're most different because we are more spontaneous than many people.

Amy: I think we're different in that we don't keep track of our age, and don't want to get old!

Pete: But we're like many other people in that we worry about finances. We may seem very care-free, but we do have a plan. It's not like we're eating all the nuts we have gathered now, and we don't have any for the winter. We're just not hoarding them. I am not afraid to go back to work, especially because it isn't really work that I do—I enjoy piloting.

*Were you ever pressured to have children?*

Amy: I know Pete's mother would have loved for us to have children. She does not understand Pete's lifestyle right now. I got subtle pressure from my parents but decided that it's not pressure unless I feel it! I'd feel worse having a child out of guilt.

*What do you see as your role in molding the next generation of children?*

Amy: It may be indirect, but not trivial—when children see us on our boat, they think what we're doing is "neat," and I tell them they could live this way when they grow up. We show them that if you work hard, have a goal, and believe you can do it, you can make your life be what you want it to be.

*Laura Carroll*

*Tell me about how you two fell in love.*

Amy: We hit it off the first time we met. I knew right away, but it took him awhile to realize it! I found Pete so adorable, funny, and fun. He had recently divorced, and friends warned me about the infamous rebound. It wasn't like that. If anything, I might have been too possessive at first, which didn't work, especially since he was just coming out of a divorce.

Pete: I knew right away that I loved Amy's independent streak. This style appealed to me because I was traveling extensively at the time.

*How did you come to buy the boat?*

Pete: We had been talking about buying a house in Florida, but I visited a friend who showed me a catamaran with modern gadgets, no wood, and I fell in love with it. Amy and I love the sun and the atmosphere that goes with it. The way I look at it, we just have a moving house.

Amy: The boat was Pete's idea. At first, I didn't feel so sure of the idea of living on a boat for part of the year. I suggested we charter a boat in Florida and, if we liked it, then talk seriously about buying one. So we did, and the first couple of days were miserable. Then the sun came, and it didn't take long before I loved the idea. When I told Pete, he said, "Good! Because I have already ordered one!"

I love having the boat, as long as I have a place to come home to. I don't think I could ever be completely portable. Since buying the boat, we have scaled down other areas of our lives. We moved into a smaller place and sold nice cars and toys, like Pete's motorcycle.

Rather than save, save, save, and then retire, we decided we'd spend it now. We wanted to live on a boat while we have the physical strength. If we waited until we're older like the norm does, then we'd have to spend the money on electric winches, and other kinds of electronic assistance to sail the boat. Now, we do all the physical things and don't have anything electronic to help us sail. It takes brut power. Older people need help doing these things.

Pete: You don't know if you're going to be ill or hobbled when you're older. I want to do this while I can.

*When you are not living on the boat, how do you spend your time?*

Amy: We work out, eat out at least three nights a week, like to go to the movies, meet up with friends, and entertain.

Pete: I run, and watch the stock market. We can live the way we do, largely because of the interest our investments are generating.

*How do you handle various aspects of the day-to-day things in marriage, for example, domestics and money management?*

Pete: Amy is the clean freak. I just stand back!

Amy: We like to go to the local farmers' market, and enjoy cooking. I tend to cook more of the "homey" things, like desserts and classic dishes, and Pete more likely gets the recipe book out to make something exotic.

Pete: With regards to money, when we were both working, we had separate accounts. For a while we had it set up so that whoever made the most money paid the mortgage, and the other one was in charge of the groceries and utilities.

Amy: As our lifestyle changed with having the boat—six months here, six months in the Bahamas, he convinced me to quit work. At first, I found it hard to give up my financial independence. I had some money for a while after I stopped working, but now I am a kept woman—and love it!

*What have been your biggest marital challenges?*

Amy: It may sound silly, but it has to be the cat. She has had her share of medical problems, and I feel for her. To Pete, it's just a cat.

Pete: We argue very little, but when we do, it's over and done in a matter of minutes. I can't think of a fight we've had that lasted more than twenty minutes.

*Many couples get married when they're ready to start a family. This wasn't the case for you. Why did you get married?*

Pete: I wanted to make the commitment. I knew I'd be gone a lot, and I wanted to know Amy would be there when I came back.

Amy: For me, the only thing that changed was my last name. The romance still goes strong!

*Families of Two*      ~ *183* ~

*How have you kept the romance alive?*

Pete: One of the greatest things about being married to Amy is–sex!

Amy: Sex is as good as, if not better than, in the beginning of our marriage. The romantic aspect of not having children is a plus! We're still spontaneous and have done it in some crazy places. If we had children, I don't think we'd be a good influence!

Pete: You have to get serious when you have children, and I don't want to do that.

Amy: I think that trust, having the freedom to do what I want to do and what we want to do also keep our marriage strong.

*As we enter a new millennium, how, if at all, do you think the institution of marriage needs to change?*

Pete: I think society needs to treat the commitment more seriously; our society makes it too easy to just get a divorce when the going gets rough. I also believe more married couples would be happier and stay together if they didn't have kids. I'd like more people to realize that they don't need to feel pressured to have children anymore. I think that men generally don't want children as much as women do. If couples waited a little longer, and took the time to learn from people who were parents, I bet we'd see even more couples choosing not to have children.

Amy: I think more couples would stay together if they waited to have them and got to know each other first. I wish society could make a law prohibiting couples from having children for the first five years of marriage. If they are not getting along or happy together at the five-year mark, the couple should not be allowed to have a child. Having a child will not make the marriage better.

Pete: I just want people to be happy and to be themselves, and having kids can stop people from being who they really are.

*Laura Carroll*

Amy: I wish that married couples would think longer and harder about having children before they jump into having them. They need to think seriously about whether they are prepared to afford them. When I see big families who don't look happy getting out of a beat up car, it saddens me.

Pete: Education is the key. Couples have to know themselves and believe they have choices in life.

# SHARYN AND PAUL

I don't feel much different than anybody else—
having kids is just a door we didn't open; that's all.
-Paul

*S*haryn and Paul have been married for twenty-one years.
They both grew up in Pittsburgh, Pennsylvania. They met
at a summer camp when Paul was seventeen and Sharyn was fourteen.
They dated though high school and college, and got married shortly
after Sharyn graduated from college.

Sharyn and Paul own a nanny agency called "Care Givers." I met
with them on a fall evening. We sat in their charming dining room
and had tea as we talked.

~

*How did you decide that you did not want children?*

Sharyn: I knew early in my life I didn't have an affinity for children.
I played with animals as a child and never had baby dolls. I am the
oldest and never enjoyed babysitting my two younger brothers and
cousins.

The steps and stages of the parenting process have never interested me. Before we got married, we decided we didn't want children.
The conversation was short. He called me in my dorm room and
asked if I wanted children. Something inside me just said, "Oh, no, I

don't want them at all." He said he didn't want them either. I was very happy to hear this!

Paul: I just seemed to know early in my life, and it never really changed. Growing up, I was not around small children. I have one older brother, and all my cousins and other relatives are older than me. Like Sharyn, the parenting process doesn't interest me. I have just never felt I needed children to fulfill my life.

*It's widely held that women have children because they are fulfilling a natural biological urge. What do you think about this?*

Sharyn: A lot of women have it, but I haven't. For a brief period of time, we tried to have kids, but I can't say we did it because I felt the maternal or biological need. In fact, I felt almost the opposite—the whole idea of being pregnant turned my stomach.

Paul: We bowed to societal pressure about nine years into our marriage. We were living and working in the Grand Canyon National Park. We didn't know what to do with our lives at the time and were looking for a change. Having a child would have created instant focus and structure to our lives. We didn't try for long. Nothing happened; we stopped trying, and we're glad we did.

*Is there anything about you or your background that you think might have influenced you not to want children?*

Sharyn: Overall, I had a very happy family. My parents had a happy and affectionate marriage. Everyone in my extended family lived near each other—my aunt lived three houses down, my grandma on the corner. We went everywhere together. We're still very close.

I know a lot of people have issues with their mother and still have children. I saw some of my mother's greatest joys and sorrows, and her kids related to a lot of her sorrows. I wasn't interested in perpetuating this.

Growing up, I felt my mother didn't accept me. I didn't feel she was ever totally pleased with me. She wanted me to be more like her—social, outgoing. I just wasn't that way, so I went my own way.

Paul: I had a good family. I don't think anything about my family background related to my desire not to have kids. I never doubted that my parents loved me. They were emotionally fulfilling parents.

I was a child who asked "why" a lot, and it drove my parents a little crazy! Maybe this characteristic had something to do with me not having children. I am not the type of person who would have "children by checklist." I had to ask myself, "Why do I really want them?" I thought the answer should be, "because I want to," not because I want to make somebody else grandparents, not because I feel expected to, or not because I could live through them. I could never come up with a reason to have them outside "I want to," and I could not say this.

*What are the biggest positives about not having children?*

Sharyn: Freedom. You can live your own life. I think we would have been good parents, but it would have meant a lot of sacrifice.

Paul: I think not having children changes one's perspective on aging. You don't feel as old when you don't have children, because you're not as focused on the changes—when four years goes by, four years go by. When you have a one year old, and four years goes by, the time perspective feels very different.

Not having children made it easier for us to start our business. It took financial sacrifices to start it, and I am not sure it would have worked if we had had children. We would have thought a lot harder about it if we were risking shelter and food for our children.

*Let's say a couple who is trying to decide whether they want children is asking your advice. What advice would you give to help them make their decision?*

Sharyn: I think it's like being in love—either you are, or you're not. With kids, we either want them, or we don't. I'd say that if they are grappling with the decision, then deep down, they probably want kids.

Paul: The grappling may have more to do with a fear of commitment, taking on such a huge responsibility, life change, or not fitting in. Underneath these issues, I bet the desire is there. If they don't have children, years later it will be hard to recoup from any regret.

Or the grappling may work another way. They may know they don't want children, but don't know how *not* to have them. We see this situation because we deal with families looking for childcare. They didn't know how not to have them, so they had them and aren't particularly happy. With a couple who is wrestling with their desire *not* to have children, I would stress that even though they may feel our society makes it difficult to choose not to have children, it doesn't mean they have to have them!

*Laura Carroll*

*What impressions do you think others have of you, as a couple that has chosen not to have children?*

Sharyn: Our families do not understand us. They are all parents, from happy families, and can't conceive of anyone who would not want to have children. We are involved with the children in our extended families, so they know that we don't mind children.

I know our families think we have a wonderful marriage. They have told us we are one of the happiest married couples they know, but I think that they think we don't know the capacity of love that they know as parents. They may think we don't know what we missed.

I think a lot of people think the only way you can experience love is with a child. To me, there are a lot of ways to give and share love, and some people don't need children to teach them this. I think that God gives us lessons to learn and different vehicles to learn them in. Relationship with children serves as one vehicle to teach people love, but not everyone has to learn this lesson in the exact same way. Not having children doesn't mean you missed the lesson.

*Do you see yourselves as different from the mainstream?*

Paul: Outside of our decision on children, and spiritual choice, I don't think we're much different than the middle class. Our families may think we're not mainstream because, in their eyes, we have done some very alternative things. We moved far away; changed our religion from Judaism to Eckankar, a non-denominational, non-Christian-based religion; worked for ten years at a national park; and didn't have children. However, we vote, pay taxes, go to work, employ people, and go to movies like "normal" people. We even drive an eleven-year-old Nissan!

*Were you ever pressured to have kids?*

Sharyn: No, not really, but we moved far away from family. We knew before we were married that we were going to leave Pittsburgh and move west.

Paul: If we had never left Pittsburgh, I'm not sure the outcome would have been the same. We may have felt more pressure. We would have remained very family-involved. In both of our families, everyone supports the kids; we all go to the soccer games, things like that. It would have been harder to break out of our childhood social strata if we lived there.

*How did your love story begin?*

Paul: I was working in the kitchen, and she was camping at a summer camp. Four days after I met her, I told her I loved her. I had never done that before.

Sharyn: I always knew we would get married. We continued seeing each other after camp even though we went to different schools. When I finished high school, I broke up with him. I told him that even though it hurt me too, I wanted to break up because we couldn't be together all of our lives if we hadn't ever been with anyone else. For about a year and a half, we still dated, but in a non-exclusive way. We saw each other and kept tabs on who the other one was dating. Paul got fed up because he thought I was playing games. Then I wanted to get back together, but he wouldn't.

I started to walk the campus and streets near his school, hoping to run into him. I even cut classes to walk around. I just wanted to be somewhere where he would run into me, and finally it worked. It took months!

*What is your life together like?*

Sharyn: We spend about twenty-three hours a day together! We don't separate our business and personal lives. If we feel like talking about work, we talk about work, if we don't, we don't.

Our work life takes up a lot of our time. We started Care Givers

*Laura Carroll*

because we wanted to be in the people business. We don't work with kids—we act as an employment agency for a particular type of job.

Paul: We're not together *all* of the time. We have separate offices and go to lunch separately.

Sharyn: It's a style thing. At lunch, Paul likes to read the newspaper, and I like to run errands.

*What do you do for fun?*

Paul: We like work to out, window shop, go to bookstores, go to the movies, hike, and travel.

*Families of Two*                    ∴ *193* ∽

Sharyn: We are involved with our church, volunteer for local theater companies, and enjoy professional basketball games. When we're home, we love to play with our cats.

*How do you handle various aspects of the day-to-day things in marriage, for example, domestics and money management?*

Paul: We easily figured these sorts of things out. We got married young and had no preconceived notions. We never had "your stuff" and "my stuff." We had albums together—that was about it!

Sharyn: We mostly split these things. I cook, and Paul does the dishes. We have a housekeeper. Whoever runs out of clothes first starts the laundry. I am better at precision measuring, and Paul is better at putting in a garbage disposal, or fixing the light. Paul does the business accounting; I do our personal bills.

*Tell me about your circle of friends.*

Paul: Most of our friends and family have children. We have no problem being flexible with friends who have kids. It doesn't bother us at all. We didn't have children because we didn't want them; it has nothing to do with anything else. Our friends can have all the children they want, and we will still be their friends.

Sharyn: We make concessions toward them, and know that for a while anyway, we have to be the ones to travel to them.

Paul: I don't think we're that different from our friends who have children. We have many of the same interests. Their main interest just takes quite a different focus for a few years. I don't feel much different than anybody else—having kids is just a door we didn't open; that's all.

*Describe your relationship with your cats.*

Paul: Our cats are our household!
Sharyn: We're crazy. I admit it!

*Laura Carroll*

Paul: I think of them as having toddlers.

Sharyn: Perpetual toddlers!

Paul: But we can leave, and someone can come in and feed them, so it is not quite the same.

Sharyn: I love animals and would love to have a dog. We don't have one because our lifestyle isn't right for it. Half of the time, we don't come home until nine o'clock p.m. That wouldn't be fair to a dog. I am not willing to do this to a dog, and I am not willing to change my lifestyle yet, but cats fit into it very easily.

We are very integrated with our cats. They eat and sleep with us. They are very interactive, and we give them a lot of love.

*Many couples talk about creating something together. Have you had similar feelings?*

Paul: We wanted to do the business because we wanted to work together. I don't necessarily look at it as a creation of something.

Sharyn: I just didn't want to spend my days with someone else's husband. It was a way to spend our time together. My parents, grandparents, and uncle's parents worked together—it was modeled for me.

*What does being happily married mean to you?*

Paul: We've always been able to grow together.

Sharyn: It means having total trust and having little turmoil. With us, everything is usually in harmony. We haven't had any difficult times, really. We have a low tolerance for feeling unhappy. We're rarely unhappy ourselves. At times, we may have been unhappy with the job, where we live, etc., but not with ourselves or each other.

*What ingredients have made your marriage work over the years?*

Paul: We both come from families that have had no divorce in any of the generations. It's never entered into our consciousness.

Sharyn: Having opposites between us has worked very well for us. I cook; he cleans. I worry; he doesn't. He procrastinates; I tend to jump right on things.

*In your opinion, how does society view the institution of marriage today?*

Paul: I think society believes in marriage as a strong institution and sees raising kids as one aspect of it. These days, it's "get married, establish your careers, have kids later." It may be later, but having kids is still an expectation of marriage.

Sharyn: Even though we didn't have children, when other relatives got married, we have normally assumed they would have children.

Paul: We never assume others are not going to have children; we assume they will. Like most people, when friends or family get married, we do the "wait and see." Then if they don't have kids, we even think to ourselves, "Maybe they can't!"

Sharyn: Many people believe there are too many divorces today. I don't necessarily think it's a bad thing if people choose to end their relationships or get divorced. I think some people don't need to stay married for a long time. It goes back to how we choose to learn our lessons in life. I think some people choose their lessons through different partners, and others choose to learn them with one person. Me—I've chosen to have my lessons with one special person.

*Laura Carroll*

# YOUR VOICE IS IMPORTANT TOO . . .

If you'd like to share your "married without children by choice" story, I'd like to hear from you. I am especially seeking couples of different ethnic and racial backgrounds who have chosen not to have children. Your voice is an important part of learning about and understanding this choice.

Email me at: laurac@inetarena.com. Thank you!

# BIBLIOGRAPHY
# AND RESOURCES

Casey, Terry. *Pride and Joy: The Lives and Passions of Women Without Children*. Hillsboro, Oregon: Beyond Words Publishing, 1998.

Ireland, Mardy. *Reconceiving Women: Separating Motherhood From Female Identity*. New York: Guilford Press, 1999.

Lafayette, Leslie. *Why Don't You Have Kids? Living a Full Life Without Parenthoood*. New York: Kensignton Books, 1995.

Offerman-Zuckerberg, Joan.(Ed). *Gender in Transition: A New Frontier* (pp. 275-284). New York: Plenum Press,1989.

Sussman, Marvin (Ed); Steinmetz Suzanne, (Ed); et al. *Handbook of Marriage and Family*. (pp.369-395). New York: Plenum Press, 1987.

# Organizations and Websites

The Childfree Association
1971 W. Lumsden Road Suite 186
Brandon FL 33511
http://www.childfree.com

No Kidding!
Box 27001
Vancouver BC Canada V5R 6A8
http://www.nokidding.bc.ca

Planned Parenthood
810 Seventh Avenue
NY NY 10019
http://plannedparenthood.org